CONTENTS

ACKNOWLEDGEMENTS   iv

CHAPTER 1   INTRODUCTION   1

CHAPTER 2   DEFINING WORK, LEISURE AND UNEMPLOYMENT   6

CHAPTER 3   EARLY SOCIOLOGICAL EXPLANATIONS OF WORK,
LEISURE AND UNEMPLOYMENT   12

CHAPTER 4   ATTITUDES TO WORK   34

CHAPTER 5   THE CHANGING CONTEXT OF WORK   50

CHAPTER 6   SOCIAL DIVISIONS AND WORK: INEQUALITY
IN THE WORKPLACE   66

CHAPTER 7   CONFLICT AT WORK   92

CHAPTER 8   UNEMPLOYMENT   101

CHAPTER 9   LEISURE   113

CHAPTER 10 THE FUTURE OF WORK, LEISURE AND UNEMPLOYMENT   130

Further Reading and Resources   142
Index   144

ACHNOWLEDGEMENTS

There are many people who support an author at the personal and professional level. Jan as always is encouraging and enthusiastic about my work and the rest of the family are tolerant of my activities. Students, past and present, are a constant inspiration for me to continue. Colleagues in the Association for the Teaching of the Social Sciences (ATSS) have often been generous in their comments which always helps my motivation.

My name is on the cover of this book but there are many unnamed 'backroom' people whose skills are essential in its production. Excellent work has been carried out by Hodder & Stoughton's Editorial team Valerie Bingham, Luke Hacker and Christopher Loades, the latter bearing much of the preparation anxieties. My thanks to everyone else who has contributed.

The Publishers would like to thank Still Pictures for permission to reproduce the photographs on pages 46 (Nigel Dickinson) and 71 (Peter Frischmuth). We would also like to thank Life File and Tim Fisher for permission to reproduce the photograph on page 71, and Photofusion and Christa Stadtler for the cover photo. Thanks to the Office for National Statistics for permission to reproduce the information from *Social Trends* (© Crown copyright 1999) on pages 84, 87 and 105.

access to sociology

WORK, LEISURE AND ECONOMIC LIFE

Nik Jorgensen

Series Editor: Paul Selfe

Hodder & Stoughton
R HEADLINE GROUP

DEDICATION

To Ami Alexandra Jorgensen, born 20th August 1998, who knows that work, play and life are all the same.

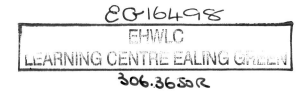
Orders: please contact Bookpoint Ltd, 39 Milton Park, Abingdon, Oxon OX14 4TD. Telephone: (44) 01235 400414, Fax: (44) 01235 400454. Lines are open from 9.00–6.00, Monday to Saturday, with a 24 hour message answering service. Email address: orders@bookpoint.co.uk

A catalogue record for this title is available from The British Library

ISBN 0 340 753 803

First published 2000
Impression number 10   9   8   7   6   5   4   3   2   1
Year   2005   2004   2003   2002   2001   2000

Cover photo from Christa Stadtler/Photofusion

Typeset by Transet Limited, Coventry, England.
Printed in Great Britain for Hodder & Stoughton Educational, a division of Hodder Headline plc, 338 Euston Road, London NW1 3BH by Redwood Books, Trowbridge, Wilts.

1

INTRODUCTION

HOW TO USE THE BOOK

EACH CHAPTER IN this book examines one or more of the central debates relating to work, leisure and economic life. The text is devised for readers with little or no background knowledge in the subject, and there are Study Points and Activities throughout to encourage a consideration of the issues raised. Student readers are advised to make use of these and answer them either on paper or in group discussion, a particularly fruitful way of learning; they will assist them to develop the skills of interpretation, analysis and evaluation. There are many ways of preparing for an exam, but a thorough understanding of the material is obviously crucial.

Each chapter is structured to give a clear understanding of the authors, concepts and issues that you need to know about. To assist understanding and facilitate later revision, it is often helpful to make concise notes.

MAKING NOTES FROM THE BOOK

Linear notes
- Bold headings establish key points: names, theories and concepts.
- Subheadings indicate details of relevant issues.
- A few numbered points list related arguments.

Diagram or pattern notes
- Use a large blank sheet of paper and write a key idea in the centre.
- Make links between this and related issues.
- Show also the connections between sub issues which share features in common.

Both systems have their advantages and disadvantages, and may take some time to perfect. Linear notes can be little more than a copy of what is already in the book and patterned notes can be confusing. But if you practise the skill, they can reduce material efficiently and concisely becoming invaluable for revision. Diagrammatic notes may be very useful for those with a strong visual memory and provide a clear overview of a whole issue, showing patterns of interconnection. The introduction of helpful drawings or a touch of humour into the format is often a good way to facilitate the recall of names, research studies and complex concepts.

Activity

Make a diagram to show the two ways of making notes with their possible advantages and disadvantages

SKILLS ADVICE

Students must develop and display certain skills for their examination and recognise which ones are being tested in a question. The clues are frequently in key words in the opening part. The skill domains are:

1 **Knowledge and understanding:** the ability to discuss the views of the main theorists; their similarities and differences; the strengths and weaknesses of evidence. To gain marks students must display this when asked to *explain, examine, suggest a method, outline reasons*.
2 **Interpretation, application and analysis:** the use of evidence in a logical, relevant way, either to show how it supports arguments or refutes them. Students must show this ability when asked *identify, use items A/B/C, draw conclusions from a table*.
3 **Evaluation:** the skill of assessing evidence in a balanced way so that logical conclusions follow. Students can recognise this skill when asked to *assess, critically examine, comment on levels of reliability, compare and contrast*, or if asked *to what extent*.

Activity

Draw an evaluation table, as below, using the whole of an A4 page. Examine studies as you proceed in your work and fill in the relevant details. Keep it for revision purposes.

Sociologist		
Title of the study	Strengths	Weaknesses
Verdict		
Judgement/justification		

REVISION ADVICE

- Keep clear notes at all times in a file or on disk (with back up copy).
- Be familiar with exam papers and their demands.
- Become familiar with key authors, their theories, their research and sociological concepts.

Activity
Make and keep **Key Concept Cards**, as shown below.

COLLECTIVE CONSCIENCE

Key idea

A term used by **Durkheim** meaning:

- The existence of a social and moral order exterior to individuals and acting upon them as an independent force.
- The shared sentiments, beliefs and values of individuals which make up the **collective conscience.**
- In **traditional societies** it forms the basis of social order.
- As societies modernise the collective conscience weakens: **mechanical solidarity** is replaced by **organic solidarity**.

Key theorist: Emile Durkheim

Syllabus area: Functionalism

EXAMINATION ADVICE

To develop an effective method of writing, answers should be:

- **Sociological:** use the language and research findings of sociologists; do not use anecdotal opinion gathered from people not involved in sociology to support arguments.

- **Adequate in length:** enough is written to obtain the marks available.
- **Interconnected** with other parts of the syllabus (such as stratification, gender, ethnicity).
- **Logical:** the answer follows from the relevant evidence.
- **Balanced:** arguments and counter arguments are weighed; references are suitable.
- **Accurate:** reliable data is obtained from many sources.

The three skill areas on p 2 should be demonstrated, so that the question is answered effectively.

In displaying knowledge, the student is not necessarily also demonstrating interpretation.

- This must be specified with phrases like 'Therefore, this study leads to the view that...'
- Sections of answers should hang together, one leading to the next. This shows how the question is being answered by a process of analysis based on the evidence.
- Reach a conclusion based on the evidence used and the interpretations made.

The skill of evaluation is often regarded (not necessarily accurately) as the most problematic. Evaluation means being judge and jury; the strengths and weaknesses of evidence is assessed and an overall judgement about its value is made. To evaluate an argument or theory, consider whether it usefully opens up debate; explains the events studied; does it have major weaknesses?

Activity

Look through some past examination papers and pick out the evaluation questions. Underline the evaluation words and work out which skills are required.

COURSEWORK ADVICE

Coursework provides an opportunity to carry out a study using primary and/or secondary data to investigate an issue of sociological interest, and must address theoretical issues. The suggestions included at the end of each chapter may be adapted or used to generate further ideas. Final decision must be agreed with a teacher or tutor.

MAKING A PLAN

Before starting a piece of coursework, you should make a plan:

1 Read and make notes from articles describing research projects in journals.
2 Have a clear aim in mind; choose an issue that interests you and is within your ability.
3 Decide more precisely what you want to know; establish a simple hypothesis to test.
4 Select a range of possible methods; consider both quantitative and qualitative.
5 Decide on a range of possible sources of information.
6 List the people to whom you can seek help, perhaps including a statistician.

WRITING THE PROJECT

1 Seek frequent advice from a teacher or tutor.
2 Check the weighting for different objectives in the marking scheme.
3 Keep clear notes throughout, including new ideas and any problems that arise.
4 Limit its length (maximum 5,000 words).
5 Label and index the study in the following way:
   a **Rationale:** a reason for choosing the subject; preliminary observations on the chosen area
   b **Context:** an outline of the theoretical and empirical context of the study
   c **Methodology:** a statement of the methodology used and reasons for selecting it
   d **Content:** presentation of the evidence and/or argument including results
   e **Evaluation:** the outcomes are weighed and strengths and weaknesses noted.
   f **Sources:** all the sources of information are listed.

OR

   a **Title**
   b **Contents**
   c **Abstract:** a brief summary of the aims, methods, findings and evaluation.
   d **Rationale**
   e **The Study**
   f **Research Diary**
   g **Bibliography**
   h **Appendix:** to include proposal for the study, single examples of a questionnaire or other data-gathering instrument and transcripts of interviews.
   i **Annex:** to include raw data gathered.

Paul Selfe
Series editor

2

DEFINING WORK, LEISURE AND UMEMPLOYMENT

Introduction

THIS CHAPTER FIRSTLY examines issues arising from defining three important areas of human societies, that is: Work, Leisure and Unemployment. All human societies have areas and activities recognisable as work and play (our leisure), but in many non-industrial societies unemployment as we know it does not exist.

If you asked a member of a pre-industrial or tribal society what they understand by such terms as work, leisure and unemployment they would probably not understand what you were talking about. For such groups life is composed of activity or doing living things, whether it be cooking, playing with children or pets, hunting and dancing. None is seen as a distinct area of life as in our society. In medieval Europe work and leisure were difficult to distinguish. What may have appeared as leisure or a pastime was often a form of rehearsal for war in a society where such conflict was frequent. Tournaments, which were equivalent to our local gala or fête days, involved archery competitions, riding, wrestling and similar activities which can be linked to martial activities. Even chess was a war game.

The language used in different societies to define work and leisure areas of life reflects this. The Dogons of Mali, for example, use the same words to describe both cultivating the ground and dancing at a religious ceremony; both (work and religious practice in our terms) are seen as useful forms of activity.

The sociology of work and leisure in industrial societies like ours focuses on:

- the significance to members of society;
- how work is compartmentalised in industrial societies as separate from the domestic 'private' sphere as well as from our leisure and 'free' time;

- work as a key aspect of our social identity and feeling of worth in society;
- attitudes to work in the light of the encroachment of machinery and technology as societies become more industrialised;
- leisure as possible compensation for boring monotonous work;
- changes in the ownership and control of business and industry resulting in ever larger corporations evolving from locally-based companies to regional, to national, to international and global corporations;
- the context of work where workplaces become increasingly larger and located in bureaucratic organisations;
- social divisions and inequality in the workplace along lines of social class, ethnicity, gender, age and disability;
- and following from this, sociological explanations of conflict at work manifested in strikes and related industrial protest;
- unemployment and its effects on people; and more recently on the impact of globalisation and related issues that will shape our working and non-working lives in the third millennium.

The topic of this book is a subject that relates to many significant aspects of our lives. The job we do or career we follow places us in society in several different ways. It relates to our class position, our standard of living, where we live, who we meet and socialise with, and even who we may fall in love with and form relationships. You may think that defining what work and leisure are is easy. Similarly what is meant by unemployment seems straightforward. However, sociologists as well as other social scientists, such as economists, point out that (as with other topics in the syllabus such as family and religion) what at first seems easy to define is not so simple on closer scientific examination. Before considering the sociological approach, let's start with your own Activity in defining the subjects covered in this book:

Activity

1   Define **1** Work, **2** Leisure, **3** Unemployment in 2–3 sentences each.
2   Compare and discuss with other students and identify common areas of agreement and areas of disagreement/controversy.
3   Devise a table to illustrate such issues.

You probably now realise that defining work,leisure and unemployment is not as straightforward as it may first seem. This chapter will consider each of these topics in turn in terms of definition and there will also be consideration of how early sociologists explained them.

WHAT IS WORK?

Gordon Marshall in *The Concise Oxford Dictionary of Sociology* (1994) defines work as 'The supply of physical, mental and emotional effort to produce goods and services for own consumption, or for consumption by others.'

This dictionary definition of work probably adds to early views that defining is not easy. Many such definitions include the idea of an economic reward for work, but does 'work' always involve an economic or financial return? The comment 'That was hard work' could apply to a range of non-financial activities including gardening, playing squash, chatting to your elderly grandma or explaining to your parent why you received a poor college or school report! However for some, such activities could be pleasurable and in the latter case understanding (or gullible!) parents could make the explanation less stressful.

WORK AND SOCIOLOGICAL IDENTITY

What do you do? Where do you work? are often the first questions we ask on meeting someone new (note: this may be less so for younger people up to the mid/late twenties for reasons we will explore later in this book). We use such information to categorise the person concerned in a range of ways. If they say a doctor or a docker, a lorry driver or a lawyer, a shop assistant or a stockbroker, we can 'pigeonhole' that person. We make assumptions about their education, their income and standard of living, the type of house and neighbourhood they live in, their hobbies and interests, their attitudes and tastes and a number of similar characteristics.

Often we are broadly correct and such is our confidence in categorising on the basis of a job title that we find that a doctor who lives in a terraced house, goes to Blackpool for holidays and reads *The Sun* newspaper is 'deviant' or strange as would be the opera-loving reader of *The Times* who drives a forklift truck in a factory.

WORK AND TIME

E.P. Thompson (1986) pointed to changing relationships between work and time as another dimension associated with changes brought about by industrialisation. In pre-industrial times work was *task-oriented*, that is you worked until a task was finished. It was also dictated by climatic and seasonal factors. So in farming, at particular times of the year seeding and harvesting can take long hours to complete, leaving quieter less demanding periods at other times of the year.

In modern industrial societies, the invention of artificial light and machines to measure time (clocks, watches) qualitatively altered work from *task* to time-*orientation* which led to the late-twentieth century description of the '9 to 5' working day.Whatever tasks need completing have to be left at 'knocking off time' until the next day. In contrast, even today in agriculture the approach to work is still dominated by daily and seasonal tasks, such as milking and planting crops.

However it can be pointed out that in an increasing number of the more professional occupations there has been a trend toward task-orientation as pressures and demands increase in a more competitive business-oriented world. Technology, notably the computer, has enhanced this by enabling work to be continued during travel to and from work, as well as at home. This clearly contradicts early conceptions of the computer as a tool to make our lives easier.

Study point

Outline some of your own examples of how computers can extend working time.

Ask professional workers of your acqaintance, eg your teachers, whether the concept of a '9–5' working day applies to them. For example how many 'take work home with them' and use personal and laptop computers outside 'normal' working hours?

WHAT IS LEISURE?

Defining 'leisure' may seem straightforward compared to the difficulties associated with defining 'work' outlined above. The origins of the word are from the French *loisir*. **David Jary** and **Julia Jary** in *The Collins Dictionary of Sociology* (1991) define leisure as:

1 the time free from work and routine domestic responsibilities and available for us in recuperation, relaxation, hobbies, recreation and cultural and artistic pursuits

2 the activities actually occupying such 'free time'.

Most dictionary definitions incorporate some idea of choice (we choose our leisure activities) and 'free' time (we engage in leisure at times when we are 'free' from work). Leisure almost always involves activity or doing, so lying on the settee may not be leisure but if you were reading a novel as well then this 'reading' may be described as your leisure. This 'action element' of leisure is clearly implied in such phrases as 'leisure activities' and 'leisure pursuits'. Many students when asked to list their leisure activities on application forms include the somewhat vague 'socialising' which is probably not specific enough for a leisure pursuit. As with the definition of work, one's idea of leisure can be relative and in the 'eye of the beholder', so what may seem inactive and 'not leisure' to some is classed as leisure for others. The American strip cartoon 'Doonesbury' featured a college dropout who became a champion suntanner, although perhaps now such a pursuit would be classed as a 'dangerous sport'!

UNEMPLOYMENT

The sociology of unemployment will be considered in detail in Chapter 8 but as with work and leisure it is worth considering issues of definition from the outset. Unemployment may seem the easiest to define, it is being out of work or not having a job as indicated by unemployment statistics. However, closer examination reveals complexities not dissimilar to those in the above sections.

One widely cited example of the definitional issues involved concerns women who stay at home with their children.They do not appear on the clearest attempt at definition of the numbers of unemployed, the Government's monthly unemployment statistics. However, it is often the case that if a suitable opportunity arose, a job would be taken up. This idea of 'opportunity' could involve childcare facilities at the workplace, suitable hours and holidays to fit in with schooling, as well as a reasonable rate of pay to make it worthwhile to go to work. Many women do not receive such opportunities so supposedly choose to stay at home but are not defined as unemployed. Other examples will be considered in Chapter 8.

Sociologists examine a number of aspects of unemployment. Some look at the effects of unemployment on individuals, groups and communities. Other studies connect unemployment with explanations of social disorganisation, such as rising crime levels, and focus on the impact of unemployment among young males in particular. Similarly, poverty and 'underclass' studies make clear links with unemployment.

SUMMARY

The three main topic areas covered in this volume raise issues of definition which can be multi-dimensional. Work, leisure and unemployment are amorphous concepts which can be defined according to economic criteria, work roles and attitudes, and social position. Each of the following chapters in this book deals with a particular dimension of the sociological approach. The main focus is on how social and historical changes have affected work and related issues through time. Sociological approaches ranging from the classical tradition to postmodernism have reflected such changes in their continually evolving explanations of an activity that is such a key feature of our lives.

Leisure as a topic has attracted increasing attention, particularly since the 1970s when the supposed increased availability of leisure for all led to descriptions such as 'the explosion of leisure'. It is now possible to study for leisure-related degrees which reflect the increased opportunities for careers in the management and provision of leisure. Leisure, sport and tourism are now multi-million pound industries employing more people than the whole of manufacturing and industry

STUDY GUIDE

Practice questions

1 Compare and contrast work in pre-industrial and industrial societies.
2 What is the difference between work that is task-oriented and work that is time-oriented?
3 'The boundaries between work,leisure and unemployment are becoming increasingly blurred.' Explain.

Coursework suggestions

1 Conduct a small survey among a group of people covering a range of ages, class and occupations, men and women, and, if possible, ethnic minorities to examine definitions of work and/or leisure. Address questions such as 'Are definitions different between the old and young? The middle and working class? Men and women?

You will need to decide on the most effective research methods for such questions. Will you use a questionnaire? Will there be open or closed questions? Formal or informal interviews?

2 An oral history project. Interview a number of older people about their working lives when they were young to cover areas such as conditions of work, hours, type of work, pay and related matters. This can provide a useful comparison with work today.

A similar activity focusing on leisure could be carried out.

3

EARLY SOCIOLOGICAL EXPLANATIONS

Introduction

THIS CHAPTER EXAMINES the contribution of three key figures in the development of Sociology: **Karl Marx** (1818–83); **Emile Durkheim** (1858–1917); and **Max Weber** (1864–1920). As founders of a subject which came to the fore in the nineteenth century as the study of industrial society, their central concern was to explain how the process of industrialisation had affected social relationships between people. Issues associated with this concerned power and inequality, the class structure and related social divisions. Work and how it became organised was a key feature of their writings and theorising. All three tended to present an evolutionary view of the development of larger, more densely populated societies with more complex forms of social organisation. Associated with such developments was the move from an agricultural to a manufacturing economy. An outcome of this was that working in fields and living in villages for the majority of the population changed to working in factories and living in towns and cities: the process of urbanisation which is closely linked to the industrialisation of society. Advances in science and technology which evolved from enlightenment thinking also contributed to a dramatic change in the way people lived and worked together. Geographical and social mobility increased dramatically. In pre-industrial societies you were born in a village, lived, married, raised children and eventually died there without travelling more than a few miles from your home.

Throughout the nineteenth and early twentieth centuries populations were uprooted from their rural birthplaces and moved to rapidly growing towns and cities. The growth of large-scale agricultural production, facilitated by technology and machinery, meant fewer workers were required, whereas there was a demand for workers in the factories and mills which burgeoned from the mid-nineteenth century on. Younger workers and their smaller, two-generational nuclear families moved away from their older relatives and their larger several-generational village families. Eventually by the late-nineteenth century there was a demand for formal education to enable workers to cope with the complexities of machinery and written instructions, measurement and recording of production which led to accounting, book-keeping and stock control, all requiring skills involving numeracy and literacy. Such developments meant that as well as geographical mobility (moving away from your place of origin) there was social mobility (moving away from your family of origin) as the educational achievements of the younger generation distanced themselves socially from their less-educated parents and grandparents. Such dramatic social changes in a relatively short space of time were bound to attract the attention and interest of scholars in the growing discipline of Sociology which became the main social science to examine and evaluate such change.

From the seventeenth century on there was a growing excitement in the potential of scientific rather than religious knowledge to explain, first, the material world of objects studied in physics and chemistry, then plants and animals studied in biology and most notably contributed to by **Charles Darwin** (1809–82). It was not surprising in such an academic and intellectual climate that a French philosopher, **Auguste Comte** (1798–1857), saw the possibility of explaining and studying the human social world in similar ways. He formulated the new discipline of Sociology which was to be the 'Science of Society', a description which is still used and debated to the present day.

It is worth noting as an introduction that the central focus in these early accounts was on European societies, predominantly British, French and German. Such a 'Eurocentric' focus has led to criticisms in the present period. These question the applicability of this analysis to all societies throughout the world, many of which have very different cultural and historical circumstances so the 'industrialisation model' cannot be applied. You will study such issues if 'World Sociology' is one of your course topics, but it is worth bearing in mind how much the issues covered in this book are applicable to a select few westernised societies, notably Britain, the USA, Germany and France. In the latter part of the twentieth century, Japan has started to feature as a comparative model for a successful advanced capitalist consumer society. Here there has been a concentration on the supposed route to economic success via sophisticated use of advanced technology, workplace organisation and harmonious management–worker relations. Reference to such issues will be made in later sections as appropriate.

Table 1: *Concepts, theories, issues and figures in this chapter*			
KEY CONCEPTS	THEORIES	KEY ISSUES	KEY FIGURES
Capitalism Class conflict Alienation	Marxism	Ownership and Control of Means of Production	Marx
Division of Labour Anomie	Functionalism	Specialisation of work Forced D of L	Durkhiem
Bureaucracy Rationality Status	Weberian	Growth in size and scale of organisations Ranking of occupations based on market situation	Weber
Managerial Revolution		Divorce between ownership and control of industry	Burnham
Stratification Meritocracy	Functionalism	Important positions filled by most talented High Salaries reflect ability and sacrifice	Davis and Moore
'Fat Cats'	Neo-Marxist	Top managers and directors making huge profits	Hobson
Industrial Society	Conflict	Use 'industrial' rather than 'capitalist' society	Dahrendorf

KARL MARX (1818—83)

It is impossible to study Sociology without understanding some of Marx's key ideas on the working of society. Your study of social class stratification, power and inequality will involve a detailed examination of such ideas. For Marx, work was an essential aspect of life in human societies; the right kind of work was essential to our humanity and sense of wellbeing. It was a natural part of human activity, an aspect of what he called our 'species being':

'the labour process is the everlasting nature-imposed condition of human existence.'

Das Kapital

It was work in a particular kind of society, capitalism, that he was most savagely critical of. Capitalist society divided people into two main class groupings: the bourgeoisie or capitalist class and the proletariat. The former owned the 'means of production' (the means that are used to produce goods and services, including the social relations between workers, technology, and other resources used). In today's terms, this would mean owners of business and industry. The proletariat, which can be translated today as the working class, do not own any aspect of the means of production. Their only 'possession' or property is their labour power which they are forced to 'sell' for wages to the capitalist. The essence of Marx's view is that this is an exploitative relationship. Capitalists make profits from the goods and services that workers produce (the technical term for the combination of such profits and overhead costs, eg heating, lighting, maintenance, is 'surplus value'). The workforce are paid wages which, for Marx, by no means reflect their contribution to the enormous wealth gained by the capitalist. In fact, they are condemned to a brutalised life of hard, remorseless toil in dangerous and physically uncomfortable conditions. They and their families lead lives of abject misery and poverty, crowded together in uncomfortable slums in unhygienic disease-ridden urban surroundings. Such conditions were highlighted by his lifelong friend and collaborator, **Friedrich Engels** (1820–95) in *Condition of the Working Class in England* (1845), an empirical study carried out in Manchester, regarded as the world's first capitalist city.

Clearly such a view cannot be disputed when such historical evidence on workers' lives in the nineteenth century is examined, but debates continue as to the applicability to workers today. One argument is that such conditions no longer prevail. Workers are paid reasonable salaries to earn a decent standard of living which, in present times, can include holidays abroad and a vast array of consumer goods such as cars, televisions and videos. Their conditions of work are vastly improved with decent surroundings, health, safety and welfare protection as well as workforce representation through trade unions. Such issues will be considered in Chapter 5.

For Marx, such nineteenth century conditions of exploitation and oppression of the majority of society would inevitably lead to conflict. As capitalism developed the larger companies would swallow up the smaller concerns, as a key aspect of the system was that to be economically successful you had to plough profits back into increasing size and scale, thus enhancing your profit-making potential. The quest for ever-increasing profits in a climate where fewer and bigger companies were in increasing competition with each other meant that wage costs were to be reduced wherever possible, thus further impoverishing workers and 'polarising' (causing a drifting apart of) the two major classes. Eventually workers would see that the only way out of their situation was to rise up and overthrow the capitalists in a political and economic revolution which would result in a social revolution where the workers took over the 'means of production' and controlled and ran things in the interests of the majority, called a 'dictatorship of the proletariat'. This would eventually mean an equal 'classless' society where everyone contributed to the economy and society, in a political and social climate summed up in Marx's famous dictum 'from each according to their ability, to each according to their needs'.

Whether or not such a society is a possibility is a subject of continuing debate, further aspects of which you will encounter in other areas of the syllabus. Briefly, critics have pointed to the ability of capitalist societies to ride through times of conflict. In the twentieth century Britain has experienced outbreaks of worker rebellion as on the eve of the First World War, the General Strike in 1926 and, more recently, the Miners' Strike of 1984. These and other similar events may have led to speculation about Marx's predictions for the demise of capitalism, but all such events have in actuality resulted in a return to more or less 'normal' conditions. Another critical aspect is the complexity of the class structure reflecting a continued division of labour according to skill and expertise, so to talk in terms of an undifferentiated homogeneous 'working class' or proletariat with common interests in the struggle against capitalists is not feasible. Some occupations require high levels of educational qualification and skills in comparison with others, which lessens the sense of a united working class. A significant number of industrial disputes around the 1970s involved workers protesting and taking action to enhance their pay differentials from those they regarded as less skilled. Also there has been the rise of a managerial group who control and run companies on behalf of their owners. They are paid a salary (wage) for this, so in strict Marxist terms are proletarian 'wage slaves'. **James Burnham** summarised this in his book *The Managerial Revolution* (1943) (see later in the chapter).

Capitalism

The Industrial Revolution dramatically changed society. The precise origins of this are still disputed by historians, but from about the sixteenth century machine technology became increasingly important as an aid to human work. This started with primitive agricultural equipment such as threshing machines for corn to make production more efficient. Wool became a major commodity for trade and industry. Technology was developed to spin yarn into thread for clothing. Inventions made such small-scale production technology as the spinning wheel, worked in people's homes, outdated and inefficient. The newer machinery was larger and had to be housed in buildings which eventually became the factories and mills we now recognise. Ownership of such 'means of production' (see above) became more important than agricultural land ownership in terms of creating wealth. Such owners, the capitalists, became the largest employers of labour, and the processes of population movements from rural to urban manufacturing areas began. This was heightened in the nineteenth century where cities like Manchester grew from small centres into vast cities within a comparatively short space of time.

A key defining aspect of capitalism is the maximisation of profit via successful business enterprise. Any profits are not used for immediate personal gratification but are ploughed back into the company to enable expansion and resultant increased profitability. Such a business milieu is extremely competitive, the aim being to grow bigger than your rivals and ultimately buy them out and take them over, adding to your size, scale and potential for increased profitability. This profit-making goal is a central source of conflict between capitalist and proletarian. The proletariat are paid wages for their labour power which is a cost which eats into the profits that the capitalist strives to maximise. It is in the capitalist's interest to keep wage bills as low as possible, whereas the worker's aim is to increase his/her wage.This conflict eventually became institutionalised via the development of trade unions and associations which represented workers' interests in their fight for higher wages and better conditions of work. This central conflictual pivot continues to the present where the source of conflict illuminated by Marx is still a key feature of our working lives. However, Marx himself foresaw that trade unions could act in the interests of capitalists by helping to curb worker unrest and encouraging the acceptance of employers' wage offers. In return modern trade union 'barons' receive high salaries (£50,000+) in comparison with their members. Some describe this as a 'sell out'.

Study point

Imagine a business owner or managing director addressing a meeting advocating that their aim was to increase the workforce's wages at the expense of profits to the company and its shareholders. Imagine a workforce advocating wage cuts to help to increase a company's profits. How would each be seen?

A fantasy situation in which so-called 'benevolent' capitalists see it to be in their interests to increase wages so workers are content and feel valued, thus increasing satisfaction and productivity which increases profits is not that remote. Correspondingly, when a firm is in difficulty workers have responded by agreeing to wage cuts or short time working.

Socialism

'Workers of the world unite, you have nothing to lose but your chains.'

This is the final stage in Marx's evolutionary model and this is where he is seen as shifting from analysis based on the type of societies which exist or have existed which can be backed by empirical historical evidence to prediction and advocacy of political action summed up in his famous rallying statement:

'Philosophers have interpreted the world, our job is to change it.'

On Marx's gravestone in Highgate Cemetery, London

Briefly explain this statement including why this view is seen as shifting from objective analysis to subjective rallying cry for political action.

Socialism is a final stage sometime in the future of industrial societies which Marx saw as inevitable. He saw the inherent conflict of capitalism described above as increasingly stretching the two major class groups apart (polarisation) like an increasingly stretching elastic band. As this band will eventually snap so will capitalism lead to revolution, as the quest for increasing profits drives the proletariat into ever-increasing poverty and deprivation. This oppressive exploitative situation leads to the heightening of political consciousness among workers as they see their future in terms of the overthrow of the capitalist system and the establishment of a society where all workers own the means of production, the 'dictatorship of the proletariat' previously mentioned. Socialism will mean a society based on equality without exploitation.This not only applies to the workplace but the whole of society. The root causes of capitalist oppression, class inequality, and alienation will no longer exist. At first the State will be required to assure a smooth transition toward full equality and democracy but eventually the need for this macro level of control and direction will 'wither away' as people become more politically aware and conscious, and able to direct their own workplace and community affairs in a truly 'communist' society.

Clearly there is much room for debate and argument in the view outlined above. Critics point to the failure of a truly socialist or communist society to emerge anywhere in the world.

Defenders of Marxism persisted that despite 'some' inequality in socialist societies:

a the extremes of wealth and poverty were nothing like as great as they were under capitalism, so a manager's salary might be double that of a worker compared to ten times in a capitalist society.

b such societies were 'classless' as by definition class only occurs where one small group (the capitalists) own the means of production and the majority (the proletariat) own nothing. In a socialist society everyone owns the means of production so there is no such thing as a class.

c similarly within the context of work alienation disappears. This is because for Marxists alienation as with class occurs in a society where the majority do not own the means of production. The Marxist sense of alienation is not just about routinised boring work tasks, it spills over into the whole of life itself under capitalism. Socialism involves the removal of alienated labour as all workers are in control of and 'own' the fruits of their labour. To use an example a worker in a British or Japanese car factory is alienated as these are capitalist societies whereas the same type of worker carrying out similar monotonous tasks on an assembly line in a socialist society is not alienated as the root causes of his/her alienation, ie non-ownership of the means of production, have been removed.

Conclusion

There is no doubt that Marx's ideas originating in the nineteenth century still have relevance to the student of Sociology. His work provided a powerful and long lasting theory of the structure and working of a particular form of industrial society, capitalism. His analysis of inequality in society based on ownership or non-ownership of the means of production is a firm basis for an understanding of class and work-related inequalities. The concept of alienation continues to provide fuel for debates concerning the possibility of worker satisfaction in a conflictual society based on exploitation of the majority by a minority. The added conflict centred around the capitalists' desire to maximise profits and minimise wage costs is a simple but highly useful model which continues to have contemporary relevance for understanding wage negotiations, industrial disputes and related industrial relations issues.

LEISURE

As previously inferred, for a Marxist, alienation does not stop at the factory gates as one leaves the workplace, so it is not enough to see alienation as purely connected with boring monotonous repetitive tasks caused by technology and machinery. Alienation's roots are concerning the relationship to the means of production. Alienation spills out of the workplace into the whole of life itself; the alienated worker is also alienated in his/her relationships to other people and at leisure or in free time is either too exhausted by the working day or takes part in mindless escapist leisure such as slumping in front of the TV, watching a diet of soap operas, quiz shows and similar non-creative, passive entertainment.

Another dimension of a Marxist analysis of leisure comes from **John Clarke** and **Chas Critcher** (1985) who see the leisure industry as another source for profit-making for the capitalist class. Large amounts of money can be made from providing escapist leisure for the proletariat to recover from their exploitative work situation.

UNEMPLOYMENT

Unemployment is seen by Marxists as an inevitable product of a capitalist system. The most frequently used explanatory model is that of the 'Reserve Army of Labour'. The driving force behind capitalism is profit maximisation and the reduction of wage costs. Marx saw capitalism as subject to periodic booms and slumps in the economic cycle. In times of economic boom profits are high, there is a demand for labour, so wage costs are higher. In times of slump profits are low, labour is shed leading to unemployment, and wage costs are reduced.

The RAL is another dimension to the capitalist process. In Marx's time he referred to them somewhat disparagingly as low-grade labourers, beggars and similar groups. This RAL can be used in times of boom to add to the labour force, helping to depress wage levels. In times of slump such groups are the first to be shed and their presence can be used as a form of threat to an insecure workforce if they are too demanding along the lines of 'If you don't like it here, there are plenty of others who can take your job'.

In summary the RAL has three main roles:

- being available as a labour force when there is a boom
- being easy to shed when times are difficult
- as a 'threat' to workers who the capitalists might see as becoming 'too greedy'.

Neo-Marxists in the twentieth century have added other features such as deskilling (Harry J Braverman, see p 44) where technology is used to replace workers and their skills helping to further reduce wage costs and add to unemployment. Such areas will be explained more fully in later sections (see pp 29–31, and Chapters 5 and 8).

EMILE DURKHEIM (1858–1917)

THE DIVISION OF LABOUR

Of the three key figures in the development of Sociology, Durkheim is most clearly seen as a sociologist as his prime focus was on the social world as distinct from that of the individual. He is often associated with a functionalist perspective in that he emphasised the holistic nature of human societies and the interconnectedness of social institutions. Following on from Comte, his advocacy of a scientific approach to the study of society combined with his famous admonition to 'consider social facts as things' links his approach to positivism, although more recent scholars have seen the straightforward link to functionalism and positivism as an over-simplification. You will study this in more detail in the theory and methods section of your course.

Durkheim's most famous work on the topic of work was *The Division of Labour in Society* (1893) and the associated concept is anomie. The division of labour in industrial societies had been studied from the time of the classical economist **Adam Smith** (1723–90) who, in his *The Wealth of Nations* (1776), had pointed to the efficiency in manufacturing productivity to be gained from dividing tasks into simple, small, repetitive activities carried out by different people specialising in that activity alone. Smith studied the manufacture of pins and saw that rather than one or a few persons carrying out all the operations from raw material to end product more efficient and faster production would come from a larger group of people, each specialising in a stage of the process.

Study point

The above points to the advantages of the increased division of labour. Can you think of any disadvantages, for example what about the workers involved in such small-scale repetitive tasks?

Durkheim recognised the inevitability of some form of division of labour as industry and associated technology grew. As did Marx he saw developments in societies in an evolutionary way. He described pre-industrial societies as bound together by mechanical solidarity. This is where such societies are analagous to a machine where people within have clear-cut roles which are recognisable and relatively unchanged through time, just like the cogs and related mechanism in a machine. So, for example, in some of the world's tribal societies all members recognise each other in terms of social and kinship relations but also as contributors in the form of 'work' roles such as fishing, hunting or making utensils. Correspondingly, personal relationships are close-knit and lifelong with a strong sense of community and belonging on the part of all. Another Durkheimian concept was collective conscience, which put simply means that there are common norms, goals and values which transcend the needs of individuals.

Industrialisation brought a dramatic change in this relatively stable and static form of society. It brings a possible threat to social solidarity and a potential undermining of the collective conscience. Durkheim used the term 'organic solidarity' to explain social relationships which were much more impersonal and short-lived, and involved larger groups of people. In the context of work, the division of labour as described developed where people increasingly specialised. Industrial societies are dynamic and ever-changing as technology advances. The associated process of urbanisation also means constant change as an increasingly migratory population shifts to places with newer opportunities. In such a society social controls cannot be at the face-to-face personal level; you need specialists such as the police to monitor and correct those who transgress and threaten social order and stability. As previously stated, Durkheim was against the forced division of labour but he saw grounds for optimism in a division of labour which involved moral consequences. Modern societies lack the common identity and sense of values (the collective conscience) that dominate pre-industrial mechanical solidarity societies, a form of loyalty to the clan or tribe. This lack of common values and clear purpose could result in a sense of lack of direction and goals to individual members which is the source of Durkheim's famous concept of anomie (the closest literal translation is normlessness). This combined with the forced division of labour could lead to class and political conflict. Durkheim's optimism came from the idea that full organic solidarity can be achieved by means of curbing unrestrained individualism and destructive competitiveness based on egotism. Such destructive anomic tendencies could be restrained by means of:

- appropriate education
- legal restraint on inheritance and other unjust contracts
- intermediary institutions to integrate individuals into occupational and industrial life.

He saw the development of the professions with associated standards and codes of ethical behaviour as a positive feature for a future society based on a complex division of labour.

MAX WEBER [1864–1920]

Max Weber was a German scholar who is regarded as one of the triumvirate who contributed to establishing Sociology as a discipline from the late-nineteenth century on. Like Marx and Durkheim, he was interested in issues associated with the nature and origins of modern industrial society. His most famous and well-known work is *The Protestant Ethic and the Spirit of Capitalism* (trans.1930), which is sometimes seen as a challenge to Marx's economic determinism which sees the economic system and technological developments as the driving force behind all social change. As the above section on Marx shows, each transistion from one stage of development to another involving agricultural and industrial 'revolutions' involves economic and technological change, such as the growth of the woollen industry and manufacturing production in factories. Weber agreed with Marx that the economic system of society was an important factor in determining social and political relations between people, and that economic position was linked to social class position, but Weber saw other factors as important also.

With regard to social change Weber disagreed that the economic 'base' was always the sole determining factor. He used the development of capitalism as a case study to highlight this. He was an expert on world religions and societies' belief systems as well as their economic and social structures. His empirical historical study of the origins of capitalism identified that it was a European development, and notably a significant proportion of early capitalists were puritan Protestants belonging to Calvinist and Lutheran sects. Their beliefs involved predestination, that God determined the course of one's life and that one's 'calling' was to live a pious and simple life involving hard work and effort at one's occupation. If this was business, then profits were a sign of earthly success, but such profits were not to be used for one's own individual lavish expenditure but were to be ploughed back in to your business and work, making for further future success. Such success was a sign from God that one's 'salvation' would eventually be reached in the afterlife. This gets around the mainstream Christian 'problem' of attitudes to wealth and riches where the Bible questions the ability of a rich person to 'enter the Kingdom of Heaven' as well as eschewing material possessions and acclaiming a life of poverty. Examples can be seen in those who enter monasteries giving up all 'worldly goods'.

For sects such as Calvinists, there is no necessity to give away 'earthly possessions' as aside from ploughing profits back into your business you live a simple abstemious lifestyle, such that these groups are often mocked by outsiders as 'tight' with money. It has been noted that in communities with a Calvinistic tradition, such as New England in the USA, parts of Holland, and Scotland, there are jokes and humour centred around the supposed miserliness of such people. Cartoon portrayals of a miser often portray someone dressed in black shabby clothing, living alone in a large draughty mansion with piles of gold hidden under a trapdoor. This could well originally link to early notions of puritanical Christians. Contemporary examples of the 'Protestant Ethic' are provided by figures such as Margaret Thatcher, married to a multi-millionaire, working a twenty-hour day in her sixties and shopping for clothes at Marks and Spencers. Sir Charles Forte, founder of the Trust House Forte hotel and catering business empire, celebrated his eightieth birthday by reducing his working week to three days. He said in an interview that he liked a fairly simple life and a pleasure for him was a Sunday meal at home with his children and grandchildren.

The 'Protestant Ethic' for Weber was the driving force behind the development of capitalism and a clear example of historical circumstances where beliefs could lead to social change. This challenges the economic determinism of Marx who thought this could not happen as beliefs, whether political or religious, always reflected the way society was organised economically. Diagrammatically the two views can be represented as:

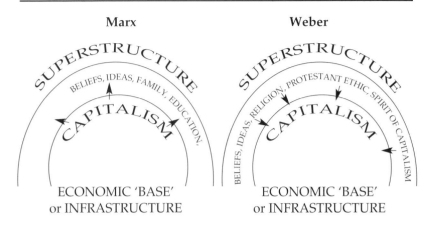

- Portrays the way capitalism affects or determines everything at the 'Superstructural' level

- Portrays the ideas in Weber's work that sometimes the superstructural level can 'determine' the way society develops economically

A COMPARISON OF MARX AND WEBER'S VIEWS ON THE ORIGINS AND DEVELOPMENT OF CAPITALISM

As further comparative evidence, Weber noted that in a number of Asian societies in the past the economic and technological circumstances were appropriate for a version of capitalism to develop but this had not occurred. He gives the example of India with its production of textiles, local guilds, merchants and trade opportunities. Weber noted that the key barrier to the development of capitalism in India was the caste system, underpinned by Hindu religious beliefs. The caste system is a static form of stratification where you are born, live and die in the same caste or group. For example, if you are the son or daughter of a dhobi or washerman/woman, you yourself are of that caste, in which you live, marry, raise children, die and pass on to your children. This goes against the requirements of capitalism for a socially mobile labour force which is adapatable to a dynamic and frequently changing economic and technological climate.

Controversy among scholars concerning Weber's thesis of the origins of capitalism continue to the present with some Marxist defenders pointing out that the early stages of capitalism were present in those societies cited by Weber before the rise to dominant social positions of Protestant sects, a version of the 'chicken and egg' view. Others (For example Marshall, 1982) point out that some European Catholic regions developed successful capitalist economies whereas even in Calvin's own birthplace, Geneva, capitalism was much slower in development, similarly in Scotland where Marshall points out the poverty of the economy as a hindering factor.

On stratification and differentiation, Weber highlighted market situation as an alternative to ownership or non-ownership of the means of production to be a key determinant of what is referred to as life chances. So, for example, a doctor (a 'wage slave' in strict Marxist terms) has a better market situation than a hospital porter. He/she earns a higher salary, has a better standard of living and an affluent middle-class lifestyle. Modern commentators see this analysis as according much closer to the complexity of the class structure in advanced societies with a complex division of labour with over 30,000 distinguishable occupations and a range of incomes from less than a £100 per week to well over £100,000 a year. Within the professions there are enormous differences in earning power and capacity as indicated in the following extract:

A winner-takes-all phenomenon – in which infinitesimal differences in ability translate into massive differences in rewards – now divides the professional class into the professional rich and the professional poor. Top barristers and accountants earn much the same as fat cats, but 15 times as much as a High Court judge, 40 times as much as a hospital consultant and 75 times what a university lecturer gets.

from *The National Wealth*, Dominic Hobson, HarperCollins, London, 1999

The workers in all such occupations in the basic Marxist sense would be deemed as proletariat or working class because they are non-owners of the means of production. Critics and advocates of Weber see this as a gross over-simplification.

Study point

Why might Marx's 'two class' model be inadequate for a modern society? Give examples of differences in 'market situation' between a solicitor and a shop assistant. How might a Marxist position be defended?

Weber was particularly interested in the process of rationalisation that underpinned the development of industrial society. Rationalisation involves a demystification of the world which is opposite to metaphysical and religious explanations and can clearly be linked to the growth of scientific knowledge and understanding. Weber further developed dimensions of the division of labour described in the previous section on Durkheim and applied it to the growth of large-scale organisations known as bureaucracies. He considered bureaucracy as a form of rational principles applied to an organisation in order to create a smooth machine-like operation similar to the working of an efficient factory. Rational division of labour involved a heirarchy of paid officials each with their own clearly defined and laid down tasks often in the written form, so no one official was irreplacable after retiring or leaving work. This was a form of authority and management of the organisation which Weber termed 'legal-rational', which compared with other forms such as 'traditional' (handed down from one generation to another, as when the boss's son or daughter takes over the firm) or 'charismatic' where authority or leadership is governed by the strength of personality or aura of the leader as in a religious sect.

A good example of a typical bureaucracy is the Civil Service where all actions are set out in written handbooks or 'Codes' for employees to consult. When seeking promotion one is advised to study such codes so they can be recited in interview. In reality such rigid adherence to so-called 'red tape' can result in inefficiency and slowness of action such that work can slow almost to a standstill. Workers in bureaucratic organisations have used this as a form of industrial action, the so-called 'work to rule' (see p 96). Such 'dysfunctions' of bureaucracy as well as further exposition of Weber's approach will be dealt with in Chapter 5.

Status

Another dimension of the stratification of society which differentiates Weber's approach from Marx concerns the way certain occupations are accorded esteem or status. As well as differing life chances and lifestyle reflecting market position, occupations receive public ranking. Many higher professional occupations command a sense of awe and deference from others. Lawyers, doctors, university professors and merchant bankers are given high status. Many people regard their doctor with a greater degree of respect than his or her receptionist.

For a Marxist such deference reflects the respect for authority that works to serve the interests of capitalism. The ruling or capitalist class do not want the mainstream 'proletariat' to question or challenge the authority of higher groups so everyday respect of higher professionals serves to maintain this. Weber saw this as overly simplistic as status was not always class-related and accorded to those with high economic position. For example, a religious cleric may have a low economic position in terms of income but people in the community give him a high social status. Similarly a poorly educated successful businessman from a working class background may not have high status despite his high economic position.

FUNCTIONALIST EXPLANATIONS OF WORK

Of the three key figures who dominated the development of Sociology from the late nineteenth century to the early twentieth century the work of Durkheim is probably closest to a functionalist view. His concept of the division of labour, so long as it is not forced, accords with functionalist ideas of harmony and integration between social institutions which can apply to the workplace. Functionalists see work as a necessary feature of all human societies, from the pre-industrial where food, clothing and shelter are the prime 'work' tasks, to complex industrial societies where a vast array of differentiated work tasks are carried out by millions of people. Work acts as an integrating force and gives meaning and purpose to life. Work relationships involve cooperative endeavour which reflects common consensual values, goals and purposes, all working together for the good of the whole.

How do functionalists explain inequalities in work when many would see them as a source of conflict? Probably the closest to a functionalist attempt at explanation of such an apparent contradiction is provided by the well-known Functionalist Theory of Stratification, first aired in a journal article in 1945 by two American sociologists, **Kingsley Davis** and **Wilbert E.Moore**.

Davis and Moore set out to provide a functionalist account of how inequality in education and eventually work operates for the benefit of the whole society. They accept that there are different abilities and talents among the population and that some occupations require high levels of skill to perform them along with long periods of education and training. If we lived in an ideal equal socialist style society everyone would earn the same regardless of skills or talents required for what they do at work. Davis and Moore's question on this is why should anyone bother with long years of study and training to be paid the same as everyone else in more unskilled work? Their key is that you need incentives which higher salaries and related rewards from work provide. The common values of the wider society accepts this, that those in highly paid work are the most able and talented and that their earlier 'sacrifices' in long periods of education obtaining qualifications such as university degrees deserve eventual reward. There is a close 'fit' between the education system and the world of work where schools, colleges and universities provide the appropriate education for the heirarchy of occupations with a range of levels of skill required to carry them out. The financial costs of particular occupations reflect a form of supply and demand where those few who are highly paid are so because it would cost more to replace them than someone unskilled, for example a surgeon could easily be trained to do a hospital porter's job whereas a hospital porter could not easily be trained to be a surgeon.

In summary, key assumptions of the functionalist theory of stratification are:

- that ability and intelligence are somewhat fixed in people from an early age
- that there is a limited 'pool' of ability and intelligence
- that schools, colleges and universities can sift out people according to their abilities
- there are common values in society where the majority accept such inequality of ability
- that highly paid occupations reflect the high skills required
- such skills require long periods of education and training and those that are able to cope with this make early career 'sacrifices' which deserve future reward.

A key concept associated with the functionalist theory of stratification is meritocracy defined as 'rule by those who possess the most ability and talent'. This is seen as a more democratic alternative to the hereditary principle where those in power pass on their position to their sons or daughters regardless of ability as with a monarchy and/or an aristocracy.

Study point

Discuss with fellow students the view that people are motivated to enter the higher professions by the prospect of high financial rewards using examples such as surgeons, lawyers and accountants. List reasons for and against.

Compare and contrast Marxist and Functionalist approaches to explaining inequality in the workplace and in access to high salaries and job satisfaction.

How would a functionalist explain unemployment?

Unemployment would be seen as a temporary phenomenon which unfortunately affected people when industrial societies were undergoing social change such as technology replacing workers in key industries. Following from Davis and Moore, they would probably highlight the role of education and retraining for unemployed workers so they could be equipped with new skills for work. So a redundant steelworker could be retrained for a job in a service industry such as driving a delivery wagon. Long-term unemployment may perhaps be explained as **Herbert J. Gans** (1972) does in *The Positive Functions of Poverty* by pointing to the number of jobs in the poverty 'industry' for administrators and social workers as a positive function(it needs to be added that some regard Gans's essay as a parody). Similarly benefits agencies employing large numbers of workers deal with the unemployed.

On consensual values and social cohesion a functionalist would argue for a level of financial support augmented by extras such as redundancy payments to be provided to enable the unemployed to continue at a reasonable standard of living, possibly stressing the temporary nature of this situation. Critics would react with horror at what they would see as a superficial 'glossing over' of a social and political problem which destroys lives, families and communities in increasing numbers. The sociology of unemployment will be addressed more fully in Chapter 8.

Leisure

This is where a functionalist would highlight the increased availability of leisure to the masses, the so-called democratisation of leisure discussed from the 1970s on. The compensatory 'function' of leisure has been identified for those in monotonous work which is an unfortunate consequence for many workers using machinery and technology. The wide availability of an enormous range of potentially stimulating leisure and sports activities which has become available compensates for unfulfilling work which is paid for by reasonable wages. Enormous sums of money – public and private – have been invested in the leisure 'industry', resulting in every town having sports and leisure complexes with motorways giving access to 'theme' parks, such as Alton Towers, attracting millions of visitors annually. The annual holiday now means access to foreign travel at a relatively low cost for the average earner. As with poverty and unemployment referred to above, the leisure industry is a major employer employing more total workers than the whole of the manufacturing industry.

THE DEBATE ABOUT OWNERSHIP AND CONTROL OF INDUSTRY

Marx saw the ownership of business and industry as being in the hands of the capitalist class, a small group of highly powerful people. Capitalists also controlled and managed their businesses being highly visible on a daily basis in their factories and mills as well as living in geographical proximity so the owner and 'boss' was a tangible figure in the workplace and the local community. This has changed dramatically throughout the twentieth century. As companies have expanded since the nineteenth century from the local 'family' firm to national and, eventually international global scale, so the question of 'ownership' has been raised. In order to raise funds for investment in expansion in scale and size of operation such companies have tended to become shareholdings where possibly thousands of shares have become available to be bought via the stockmarket. The result has been that there has been a decline in 'family' ownership and an increased 'spread' of ownership to large numbers of shareholders who are the new 'owning' class. Shareholders have the right to attend annual general meetings and vote on issues of company policy and direction. However it has been pointed out that such 'ownership' and influence in company affairs is illusory.

Major decisions of company policy and direction are invariably made by boards of directors who are often majority shareholders who can outvote ordinary members if rare conflicts arise. Such directors could well be family descendants of original owners, for example Sir Charles Forte passed on his controlling influence and managing directorship to his son Rocco with his daughter-in-law also being involved.

The 'Fat Cats' Scandal

One reason businessmen now pay themselves a lot is that they can: directors of the modern plc are in a uniquely favourable position. They do not own the company but they control its resources. Like most people in charge of money that belongs to someone else, company directors are naturally tempted to bestow it on themselves.

from Dominic Hobson, *The National Wealth* (1999)

A recent issue concerning Boards of Directors is that through the 1990s they have had the power to vote themselves large salary increases, as well as bonus payments often totalling thousands of pounds and generous 'severance' packages on leaving, some as high as £1 million plus, regardless of whether the company had recently been profitable. This led to the attention of the media with their focus on the so-called 'fat cats'.

It is safe to say that no director of a FTSE 100 Company* is getting less than £180,000 a year. At the largest companies, no member of the board is taking home less than £250,000 a year, and the highest paid directors are collecting well over £1 million. It is reasonable to assume that, in an average year, the highest-paid directors at FTSE 100 companies will be earning between £600,000 and £1.5 million a year. Earning more than £1 million is commonplace in the City and is no longer unusual in industry and commerce. A 1998 survey of the top 350 British companies identified 49 directors who earned more than £1 million.

from Dominic Hobson, *The National Wealth* (HarperCollins, London, 1999)

*Financial Times-Stock Exchange 100 share index, an index based on the share values of Britain's 100 largest companies set up in 1984

Public attention to this via the mass media was heightened in the late 1990s, many agreeing with the sentiment in the following extract from a speech by John Edmonds, general secretary of the GMB general union, at the 1998 TUC Conference:

A company director who takes a pay rise of £50000 when the rest of the workforce is getting a few hundred is not part of some general trend, he is a greedy bastard.

In the summer of 1999, the Labour government proposed that shareholders should have greater voting rights and the power of veto over such profligate increases but it remains to be seen how effective this might be.

Activity

Company directors are 'greedy bastards' How would **a** Davis and Moore and **b** a Marxist respond to and explain this view? Write short notes based on your reading from previous sections.

THE MANAGERIAL TRADITION

This was highlighted early in the twentieth century through the work of management theorists such as James Burnham (1942) who pointed to the growth of salaried company managers who ran companies on behalf of their capitalist owners. This is sometimes referred to as the divorce between ownership and control. This developed as a result of the growth in size, scale and complexity of work organisations where specialisation and an increasingly complex division of labour coupled by advances and implementation of technology meant that the 'one man' business owner was a thing of the past. Managers themselves had to specialise in a wide range of areas so personnel management, production and works managers, accountancy and financial managers became separate professions, eventually with their own qualifications and professional associations and licences to practice. In the latter part of the twentieth century the use of computing technology added further to the complexity of operations in running a company. Burnham considered that managers acted in their own professional interests, whereas **Adolf Berle** and **Gardiner Means** (1933) saw managers acting with a broader social conscience guided by professional values. Such views were seen as a challenge to orthodox Marxism where different arenas for conflict around new authority relationships were seen to emerge replacing those around employer-employee relations (**Ralf Dahrendorf**, 1959).

More recent studies have questioned the assumed professional neutrality of managers. Marxist influenced theorists such as **M Useem** (1984), while accepting that managers could be seen as proletarian 'wage slaves', have pointed to the commonality of interests between management and owners, in that managers are employed to improve productivity and profitability and keep wage costs down. For this they receive a much higher salary than shopfloor workers. In other words, ideologically they are on the side of the capitalists.

The Emergence of the Manager/Director Distinction
Later twentieth century developments in shareholding have brought in the opportunity for senior managers and board directors to be rewarded with shares as part of their salary 'package' (see 'fat cats' debate above, p 29–30). This clearly raises issues of ownership particularly when such managers become majority shareholders. In recent years there have been clearer heirarchical and qualitative distinctions between directors and managers with the latter running the day-to-day administrative and production aspects and directors involved in the more strategic and policy-making aspects of the company. To take a specific example, the manager of a supermarket is paid to run that particular branch in terms of ordering stock, staff supervision, training and recruitment, customer relations and similar activities; whereas the board of directors of that supermarket chain will rarely enter one of their branches, and will work in sumptuous city offices making strategic and policy decisions concerning the overall company. One example of such a policy decision in the late 1990s was that of Sainsburys and Tescos to open small town centre branches in preference to further out-of-town hypermarket developments. This reflected political developments in transport policy where governments are concerned about reducing traffic and encouraging the redevelopment of pedestrianised city centres.

Study point

If you have a part-time job, observe and note the work of a 'manager' in the light of the above. What sort of tasks does management involve? To whom is the manager responsible? Where do their loyalties lie? To the employees? or, to a higher authority? (identify).

Activity

Write a short essay:

'Managers are the servants of the capitalist ruling class'. Discuss.

SUMMARY

This chapter has discussed the classic sociological studies on work, leisure and unemployment from Marx, Durkheim and Weber who focused on the early development of industrial societies in the nineteenth Century. Features highlighted were:

- the nature of capitalism and its origins
- the increased complexity of the division of labour in industrial society
- associated changes in attitudes to work explored through concepts such as alienation and anomie
- the growth in scale and size of work organisations.

More recently, such features as:

- the positive 'functions' of work in a society with collective goals and values
- the debate about ownership and control of industry
- the managerial revolution
- the shift from primary, extractive industries to secondary manufacturing, to tertiary service and distributive industries and associated qualitative changes in work roles

have increased our knowledge of such a rapidly changing and vitally important area of our lives. The theories and ideas of Marx, Durkheim and Weber addressed important issues associated with industrialisation and the way work has changed in recent times. Their work is still seen as relevant and is the subject of continuing debate to the present day.

STUDY GUIDE

Group work

Three groups each to choose one of Marx, Durkheim and Weber. Research their approach to industrialisation and in particular the topic of work. Write up and prepare a class handout or display poster. Set up a debate where one from each group gets in role, gives a 10-minute talk on their key ideas and is then questioned by the role player from the other two groups. Questioning can then be opened to the rest of the class. After the three 'founders' have finished, class to vote on which has the most to contribute to an understanding of work in our present times.

Practice questions

1 Compare and contrast the analysis of work in an industrial society of any two of the following: Durkheim, Marx and Weber.
2 'It is the process of industrialisation rather than capitalism which best explains the modern world of work.' Discuss.

Coursework suggestions

1 Select any one classical sociologist or an approach such as functionalism and construct a research project to investigate the modern applicability of their theories on the nature of work in industrial societies. For example:
Is Marx's view of alienated work applicable to workers today?

2 Examine a range of occupations to see if their 'market situation' (Weber) is a factor in areas such as pay, conditions and work satisfaction.

4

ATTITUDES TO WORK

Introduction

THE PREVIOUS CHAPTER considered some of the early sociological explanations of work and leisure in industrial societies which were developed in the nineteenth century. A dominant view was that work for the majority in mechanised production in factories and mills had become increasingly dissatisfying. Technological developments had increased the mechanisation of industry to such an extent that most such workers had become 'appendages or slaves to the machine'.

In this chapter we will examine whether such a predominantly negative view can apply to the whole of work in an industrial society such as ours. Commonsense and a range of sociological studies suggest that attitudes to work are more complex than this negative view implies. Even within the same type of occupation different workers may have a wide range of attitudes from intense dislike to a love of the work.

Table 2: *Concepts, theories, issues and figures in this chapter*			
KEY CONCEPTS	THEORIES	KEY ISSUES	KEY FIGURES
Dual labour markets	Labour Market	There are primary and secondary employers	Barron and Norris
Life chances	Weberian	Job and pay reflects market situation	Weber
Alienation	Marxism	The worker is estranged from the product of his/her labour	Marx

KEY CONCEPTS	THEORIES	KEY ISSUES	KEY FIGURES
Technological Determinism		Alienation levels vary according to technology	Blauner
Instrumentalism	Neo-Weberian	Work is seen as a means to an end, so boredom endured	Goldthorpe and Lockwood
Social determinism		Different industries can be differentially affected by social and technological factors at work	Wedderburn and Crompton
Alienation	Neo-Marxist	The pressures on car assembly lines	Huw Beynon
		Work in high tech chemical industry still alienates workers	Nichols and Beynon
Deskilling	Neo-Marxist	As capitalism has evolved technology has been used to replace workers' skills	Braverman
Skill	Feminist	'Skill' defined by men, women's skills ignored or undermined	Beechey
	Feminist	Female clerical workers exploited in low-paid work	Crompton and Jones

At the commonsense level it may seem that considerations over whether work is satisfying or dissatisfying to people depends on the job or occupation. It appears that some jobs are routine and boring because they involve repetitive and simple tasks which are not fulfilling – the well-known 'I could do this in my sleep', or as a respondent in a social survey said, 'a monkey could do what I do' apply to such jobs. Most consider factory work to be of this nature, particularly of the type which involves assembly line production. Such jobs in food processing as stripping meat off chicken carcases as they pass on a conveyor belt, or putting hub nuts on car wheels are examples.

However, there is also the view that a large number of occupations are not of this kind. They are involving and fulfilling, and satisfying in the levels of creativity and aptitude they require. Most would consider professional occupations such as doctors, teachers, lawyers and journalists in this way. It needs to be noted that as well as satisfaction from the work tasks themselves (intrinsic) which often involve thinking and problem solving, there are also related dimensions of satisfaction to be gained from being in control of your work (autonomy) rather than controlled and supervised by machines or supervisors on an assembly line. Other external (extrinsic) satisfying dimensions come from high salaries and status within society. Compare being able to tell someone you are a lawyer to telling someone you are a factory worker.

One sociological approach that suggests that most occupations in the late twentieth century have become comparable with the professions in that they are becoming more satisfying is the functionalist theory of stratification (see Chapter 3). This approach identifies the need for an increasingly educated and intelligent work force to cope with the demands of a more complicated technologically advanced work environment for the majority (see below). Associated with this is the view that work will become increasingly involved with the need for creativity and flexibility in approach, key factors that make work more interesting and satisfying.

For a long while sociologists have echoed public perceptions of work satisfaction in that boring work is most often associated with manual or working class occupations (referred to in America as 'blue collar' workers) and more satisfying work is more likely in non-manual middle class occupations ('white collar' workers).

More recently issues of gender and ethnicity have been added to the traditional social class analysis pointing to the large proportion of women and ethnic minority workers in less satisfying jobs, particularly in white collar fields such as clerical and shopwork, thus challenging earlier ideas that boring work was usually manual. Another dimension to this is an increased blurring of the manual/non-manual divide in terms of the possibility of dissatisfying routine monotonous work. For example, in the late nineteenth century clerical occupations were clearly middle class with better pay and use of skills of literacy and numeracy than most manual work. Compare this to clerical work today where the lower grade tasks are every bit as mundane and repetitive as the most boring factory job. The fact that such clerical occupations are mainly occupied by women – often part time because of home and family commitments – has been highlighted by feminist writers since the early 1970s. More recently, similar points have been made concerning ethnic minorities where discriminatory practices have forced many into less satisfying work below their educational levels and qualifications.

Such issues will be considered in more detail in Chapter 5 but it is worth noting the link to the idea of a 'dual market for labour' (**R.D. Barron** and **G.M. Norris** (1976). This theory suggests that there are two 'labour markets' for employment:

1 The 'primary' labour market concerns large profitable companies who dominate their business and product markets. They can offer secure well-paid employment with prospects for promotion and advancement. Examples of this type of company are Ford Motors (cars), the Sony Corporation

(electronics) and Unilever (chemicals). The predominant type of worker is young, white and male, working in an involving satisfying job in pleasant surroundings.

2   The 'secondary' labour market involves small firms in an insecure, volatile business environment. Firms offer lower pay and often temporary part-time work so labour can be easily shed in difficult times. There are few opportunities for advancement and work is likely to be routine and unfulfilling. Examples of such firms are the so-called 'backstreet sweatshops' producing cheap clothing and similar goods. These firms are major employers of unskilled women and ethnic minorities, as well as vulnerable groups such as old people and the disabled. As you would expect, work in the former firms involves positive attitudes and in the latter, more negative attitudes.

Activity

Conduct a small survey either **a** in your own neighbourhood to identify primary and secondary labour market firms to see if the above model applies. What type of worker do the different types employ? or **b** among employed relatives and acquaintances to see how their occupations accord to such labour markets, eg are women factory workers in more insecure, unsatisfying work than men?

ATTITUDES TO WORK FROM A WEBERIAN PERSPECTIVE

Some of the main ideas evolving from Max Weber with relation to work in an industrial society have been outlined in the previous chapter. Higher market position, for example a professional person, meant higher social standing accompanied by higher salaries and better life chances than those in more unskilled occupations. Although not clearly spelt out in Weber's writings, the implication is that those in higher occupational positions would also gain greater satisfaction from their work. Such work is more involving and has complexity and variety requiring higher educational levels.

However, another dimension to Weber's work concerned the growth of large-scale bureaucracy which would gradually spread to most work environments. The negative aspects of this have been referred to previously, where Weber painted a somewhat gloomy picture of an 'iron cage' entrapping increasing numbers of workers in a network of inflexible formal rules and procedures, stifling creativity and freedom of action. Increased bureaucratisation would not only affect workplaces but spread to the whole of society. We can perhaps see evidence of this in our current times where it seems that much of our everyday lives is spent in negotiating bureaucracy, whether it is ordering a train ticket, applying for a passport, querying a bill or returning faulty goods.

On balance it would seem that the picture to be drawn from Weber's work is somewhat mixed. It is true that bureaucracy has encroached on many aspects of our lives and that work within bureaucratic organisations can be dissatisfying and routine. But as modern organisational theorists have pointed out, there are a range of responses to this such that an informal structure often develops where workers dictate what gets done and how, key elements in job satisfaction.

MARXIST APPROACHES TO UNDERSTANDING SATISFACTION AT WORK

The idea espoused in the previous section that there is a heirarchy of satisfaction with professional and similar occupations having higher levels than routine manual work is challenged by Marxism which suggests that such a view is illusory. While accepting that some middle-class occupations might be more rewarding, all work in a capitalist society involves the exploitation of those who do not own the means of production, that is the proletariat or working class, by the bourgeoisie, the owners of the means of production. Such exploitation affects all, regardless of occupation, and is the cause of alienation, which results in dissatisfaction with work for all, albeit at different levels depending on the occupation.

Marx applied the concepts of alienation and class conflict produced in the workplace of a capitalist society to an explanation of how such conflicting social relations of production will eventually lead to revolution and the end of unfulfilling work. So what at first is a negative account of work in a capitalist society contains the seeds for optimism in the future.

Marxists throughout the twentieth century have continued to develop the basic tenets of Marx's negative views of work in a capitalist society, particularly developing the concept of alienation and applying it to our understanding of work.

MODERN TRENDS IN ALIENATION – LATE TWENTIETH CENTURY ATTACKS ON THE PROFESSIONS

Another modern dimension to this is that as capitalism evolves, the constant quest for increased profitability means there is pressure for higher productivity on all workers. This combined with increased managerial control and political attacks on the independence of the professions (started in the early 1980s with Thatcherism) resulted in increased numbers of once autonomous occupations being supervised and directed from above. This is a significant factor in a decline in job satisfaction in all walks of life. Teaching provides a good example of this. Up to the 1970s teachers were highly regarded professionals with relatively high status combined with autonomy in their work, key factors in job satisfaction. The trends described above have changed this dramatically. New contracts of employment were drawn up with increased hours and precise stipulation of duties. The setting up of OFSTED in the early 1990s, a government inspection agency, along with league tables of schools' performance, has brought the teaching profession into the public domain much more. This may seem to be a good thing; a sign of democracy and openness making teachers more accountable. However, the effect has been to create a sense of 'threat', which combined with the stresses of regular inspections, newspaper highlighting of failing schools and longer hours of work has eroded work satisfaction for a large number of teachers. In the late 1990s the government introduced a policy of pay differentials with so-called 'super-teachers' commanding higher salaries than the rest. This could be seen as further adding to the burden of demands on teachers who are not so rewarded, further undermining confidence and satisfaction in work. Similar trends have occurred affecting all the professions including doctors (league tables of hospitals and surgery), nurses (high pay for 'super-nurses') and the police (league tables of crime clear up rates).

Another dimension from a Marxist perspective is provided by the 'Deskilling' debate (see below). Here, whenever possible, technology is brought in to supplant the skills of workers who can either be dispensed with (this is *Automation* where machines take over completely as with robots assembling cars) or replaced by less skilled workers who operate the machine (*Mechanisation*), an example being a craftsman welder being replaced by a welding machine operated by a semi-skilled worker.

In the late twentieth century increased computerisation meant that deskilling spread to non-manual and professional occupations. At the time of writing the British government is proposing self-diagnosis for patients via the Internet. If you are ill, you can describe your symptoms to your computer which will diagnose and prescribe, saving you a visit to your GP. Clearly such trends are there to supposedly improve efficiency with technology but another effect is to save money and replace workers, further undermining professional autonomy and work satisfaction.

In summary, a Marxist would point to such trends as an inevitable outcome of capitalist aims to undermine the power and control of all occupations, thus cheapening labour costs and increasing profits for the ruling class. One clear outcome is a decline in job satisfaction and a growth in alienation affecting all occupational groups as the above case study of the teaching profession shows.

Study point

Imagine if your Sociology course was conducted by computer. What differences would there be? Would it be possible? What might be the advantages? What are the disadvantages?

Activity

Write a short passage addressing whether work in the future will become increasingly computerised, covering arguments for and against.

TECHNOLOGICAL DETERMINISM

Alienation and Freedom by **Robert Blauner** (1964) was an early empirical study carried out in America in the late 1940s. He set out to examine alienation at work in a range of industries including printing, textiles, car manufacture and chemicals. Unlike Marxist predictions of increased alienation for all workers as capitalism developed, Blauner found that levels of alienation varied according to the technology used and the levels of skill required. The least alienated workers were in the printing industry where work involved high levels of craftsmanship, leading to a sense of satisfaction and fulfillment. The most alienated were in the car industry where technology had reduced work to simple repetitive tasks. Blauner's prediction was an optimistic one that industries such as printing would continue their demand for skilled workers and less skilled work would be replaced by machines. At that time he did not envisage that computerised developments in printing would lead to a decline in the demand for craft workers along the lines predicted by Marxist-influenced writers. Also that the inexorable encroachment of technology in the workplace would lead to higher levels of dissatisfaction for the majority.

Another prediction was that more technology, as in the chemical industry would require a higher skilled workforce leading to less alienation. For another view see **Theo Nichols** and **Huw Beynon** below (p 44) who question Blauner's assumptions, seeing similarities between the chemical industry and other types of industrial factory work.

Blauner's approach became known as Technological Determinism because of the focus on the key role of technology in creating satisfaction/dissatisfaction at work. Alienation at work was a product of the production technology used, a narrower definition than that of Marxism (see p 18). For Blauner an alienated worker in a car factory could be in a socialist or capitalist society; his or her situation is a product of the car building technology and machinery used.

Study point
Evaluate the views above. Is it possible to create job satisfaction by **a** changing the work and technology used, or **b** changing society from capitalism to socialism? Outline the strengths and weaknesses of each.

Keith Grint (1992) criticises Blauner's work for:

- having dubious data sources which were in fact gathered for other purposes, were dated and contained leading questions on job satisfaction;
- generalising all workers' use of technology and operations in a particular industry such as printing as similar when a variety of tasks and skills are involved;
- assuming that issues of ownership and major decision-making powers are unimportant when in fact they can be seen as key dimensions of alienation at work;
- sometimes focusing on external factors such as community bonds as reducing alienation, as cited for textile workers, when his theory focuses on an internal factor, the role of technology in affecting levels of alienation;
- contradicting his theory connecting alienation solely with technology by recognising that a key factor in fatigue and levels of satisfaction for women was their dual role as domestic and textile workers, showing that factors other than technology need to be considered.

THE AFFLUENT WORKER DEBATE

Some of the problems with technological determinism as put forward in Blauner's study highlight its one-dimensional or monocausal nature, that is technology is the main explanatory variable concerning work satisfaction. Later writers saw the limitations of this and pointed to the complexity of factors involved. A famous British study was carried out in the car industry in the early 1960s and became known as 'the Affluent Worker' study (1968). Among the report's co-authors were two eminent British sociologists, John Goldthorpe and David Lockwood, who were experts in the field of social stratification. The study originally set out to test the 'embourgeoisement thesis' which suggested that in post-Second World War Britain there had been rising levels of affluence, incomes and prosperity affecting all working groups. This had led to a breaking down of traditional class divides between manual and non-manual workers, summed up in the statement, 'We are all middle class now'. It is worth noting that there are modern equivalents of this view in the then Prime Minister, John Major's espousal of a classless Britain, a theme taken up by the New Labour government as part of their ideas of a 'Third Way' and their appeal to 'Middle England'.

The 'Affluent Worker' study seriously challenged the embourgeoisement view finding clear distinctions continuing between middle- and working-class workers on a range of measures including class identity (highly paid car factory workers still saw themselves as working class despite good standards of living) and voting behaviour (the majority still voted Labour and saw this as the party for the working class). One key feature that emerged from the study concerned attitudes to work. Most of the car factory jobs were relatively low-skilled, routine and monotonous, a clear example of alienated dissatisfying work. However, rather than as would be thought if the line of technological determinism was followed, such workers did not leave for other available jobs requiring more involvement and skill. Rather they stayed for other reasons, most significantly the good money to be earned in such a high-paid industry which gave them the means to a good standard of living including their own houses, cars, holidays and a range of consumer goods. Goldthorpe and Lockwood termed this the 'instrumental orientation to work'. Such carworkers saw work as a means (money) to an end (high standard of living). This was an external or extrinsic factor as compared to technology which was an internal or intrinsic factor in satisfaction with work. The Affluent Worker study became associated with social determinism, that is outside social factors such as the desire for a good standard of living superceded any factors such as the nature of work itself.

Later studies added further complexities to the ideas of technological or social determinism. **Dorothy Wedderburn** and **Rosemary Crompton** (1976) found that both could apply depending on circumstances. They studied a variety of industries and found that levels of job satisfaction between industries varied as expected (Blauner) and technology could lead to more skilled satisfying work. In other industries instrumental orientation applied where workers resisted managerial attempts to make monotonous work more varied and interesting if this was perceived as a threat to levels of pay and bonuses.

Duncan Gallie (1978) carried out a comparative study of British and French oil refineries where the same technologies were used. If technological determinism was correct, it would be expected that attitudes to work and levels of satisfaction were similar in Britain and France. This was not the case with more dissatisfaction being indicated by French workers in terms of oppositional attitudes to management ('them' and 'us') and involvement in industrial disputes as well as verbally expressing dislike for their work. Gallie's conclusion concerned cultural and political differences between British and French society. France has a revolutionary history and is a republic, whereas Britain has not had a major political revolution and is a monarchy. Gallie concluded that the British working class is more derefential and possibly grudgingly accepting of their lot in terms of work and expressions of satisfaction. The French working class are much more politicised and willing to take part in action such as street protest in order to register their dissatisfaction. Clearly Gallie offers a more socially deterministic view adding dimensions of history, culture and politics to the complexity of our understanding of attitudes to work initially addressed in the early studies of Blauner, and Goldthorpe and Lockwood.

TECHNOLOGY AS A CAUSE FOR OPTIMISM?

Some more optimistic functionalist writers followed on from Davis and Moore (see p 27) predicting that an increasingly educated and skilled workforce would be needed to cope with the demands in the workplace as technology advanced. This contains the assumption that work for the majority would become more satisfying.

A different view which also contains a positive element in explaining attitudes to work came from functionalist sociologists who saw the increased lack of fulfilment from work for many as an inevitable, if regrettable, price to pay for the benefits from increased production to the whole of society. Massive increases in production throughout the twentieth century has brought increased availability of an enormous range of consumption goods and increased standards of living to levels unimagined by our forebears. This is supported by regular consumption surveys showing the increased ownership per household of a massive array of goods such as cars, TVs and videos, Hi-Fi and CD equipment, as well as domestic appliances such as dishwashers, fridges, freezers, microwaves and washing machines. All such products are made in factories where work has become increasingly mundane and repetitive. For a functionalist compensation for this comes from reasonable pay which in turn gives access to such goods thus improving standards of living and a sense of wellbeing. Further compensation from enjoyable leisure and holidays means that the '9–5 slavery' of a large number of workers has become a means to an end, a cost outweighed by the advantages gained.

However, most sociological studies of the workplace highlight the negative dimensions of work in advanced industrial societies. A range of empirical studies of factory work throughout the twentieth century have exposed what working with machines and on assembly lines is like for many workers. Some are Marxist-influenced such as Huw Beynon's *Working for Ford* (1973) an observational study of a Liverpool car factory. Beynon found that such work on assembly lines was oppressive and demanding and high levels of dissatisfaction were expressed. The Marxist view of a worsening situation was supported as demands for increased productivity in a highly competitive market led to an increase in the pace of the assembly line instigated by management. Such a pressurised situation for the workers could lead to sick humour such as the nickname 'heart attack machine' for a machine that had actually resulted in coronaries for operators due to the demanding pace and stress involved.

In *Living with Capitalism*, Nichols and Beynon (1977) give an account of their study of a chemical plant to examine if, as had often been suggested, work in a highly automated technological industry was improved as some functionalists had predicted. It was assumed that highly skilled technicians in clean white coats would be the highly paid benefactors of such new forms of technologised work. They found little evidence of this; one area of the plant was nicknamed the 'Black Hole' because of the dark clouds of chemical dust that obscured the light. Masks had to be worn and breathing was difficult in conditions that rivalled those found by Marx in chemical factories in nineteenth century London. Technology had not made work lighter, there were still heavy labouring and lifting jobs to be carried out by significant numbers of workers. The only 'benefits' of technology were to management who could, where possible with fuller automation, shed skilled highly-paid workers and employ many fewer unskilled 'machine minders'. Needless to say, the majority of the chemical workers in this study were dissatisfied with their work.

THE DESKILLING DEBATE

This has provided a major challenge to a number of the approaches examined in previous sections. The major proponent of deskilling is the American Neo-Marxist, **Harry J. Braverman**, whose *Labour and Monopoly Capital; the Degradation of Work in the Twentieth Century* continues to attract attention since its first publication in 1974. Braverman offered a historical study of changes in American industries from early industrialisation to their dominance as world's foremost industrial producer of the twentieth century continuing to the present. Braverman's study showed a decline since the nineteenth century in craftsman occupations where technology was used, but often as tools were made by the worker, a high level of skill was used adopting such tools to aid in producing goods. Clearly such workers were powerful. Managers had to accommodate to them and fulfill their demands as skilled craftsmen are not easily replaceable. Increased mechanisation and eventually automation gradually replaced the need for craft skills. Such developments changed the balance of power in favour of the capitalist whose ideal was to deskill as many workers as possible so they were relatively unskilled and could be paid less, and would have to put up with whatever was offered. Thus the interests of profit maximisation were enhanced by replacing the skill of the worker by the machine. Unlike workers, machines do not have to be paid and can be worked for 24 hours per day, all year round if necessary. The ultimate stage in mechanisation is the fully automated factory where few, if any, workers are necessary. Some car firms in Japan have come very close to this with the use of robot technology replacing people in virtually every part of the production process.

ROBOTS REPLACE WORKERS ON A CAR PRODUCTION LINE

This idea of machines taking over and replacing skilled workers has appeal and a certain logic in terms of the capitalist system. It certainly seems true that there are fewer craftsmen and women in a lot of industries, with engineering being a good example. For much of the twentieth century engineering factories employed a wide range of highly skilled craftsmen, many operating complex machines, such as centre lathe turners and toolmakers. Such workers served up to seven-year apprenticeships and had to study for appropriate qualifications on day release and at night school. When their 'time' or apprenticeship was completed there were often elaborate ritualistic ceremonies to celebrate their progression to a new high earning status. For many males this became a form of 'rite of passage' into adult manhood with accompanying expectations such as marriage and having a family. Up to the 1970s such workers were in demand and had secure well paid employment for life. This has now changed with many features of Braverman's deskilling argument evident. Ever more sophisticated machinery has replaced such early craft jobs.

Not surprisingly Braverman's thesis has attracted attention and criticism. The following are some of the main ones:

- over-generalisation – it is true that 'deskilling' has affected a diverse range of industries where many jobs have become less skilled and machinery and automation have replaced workers. However, there are a number of examples where technology has meant that jobs have been 'reskilled' or 'enskilled'. The work of the conventional secretary/typist operating a typewriter has changed dramatically such that a high level of computer ability is required and such workers have been retitled as adminstrators, data processors and office managers. The nurse today has to be knowledgable about a wide range of medical advances and changes in patient care as well as being able to deal with ethical issues such as euthanasia. Similarly police work has become more complex with the use of computers and the demands of a diverse and rapidly changing society.

Empirical studies of today's industries have also led to questioning of the wholesale acceptance of deskilling.

Roger Penn (1984) found little support for Braverman in the paper industry where labouring had declined as a result of mechanisation such as fork lift trucks requiring more skilled workers.

GENDERED DIVISION OF LABOUR IN THE THIRD WORLD: TECHNOLOGY TENDS TO BE USED BY MEN

- historical inaccuracy – a 'golden age' of artisans and craft workers? Critics say that Braverman over-emphasised the proportion and significance of highly skilled craft and trades workers in the nineteenth century. There were many unskilled labourers and casual workers who had far more insecure work conditions and less rights than those affecting such workers today.
- feminists such as **Veronica Beechey** (1982) have added to the debate pointing out that 'deskilling' has affected women workers more than men. Where technology is used it tends to be men who operate it as women do low skilled work. In the developing world it is notable that much basic labouring is carried out by women while men operate large machines such as earth movers and diggers.
- Gallie (1994) adds the element of 'skill polarisation', suggesting that those jobs with high level skills are becoming more complex and those with low level skills are becoming deskilled or replaced by machinery. Such a process of 'selective deskilling' is adding to the existing divisions in society. Again feminists have pointed to the gender inequality of such a process. **Rosemary Crompton** and **Gareth Jones** (1984) studied clerical workers and found in the banking and insurance industries that the lower grade occupations mainly done by women were being deskilled and that higher grade work was mainly carried out by men. Sometimes employers exploit gender and other social divisions such as ethnicity, by employing less unionised, unskilled female and ethnic minority workers in preference to skilled, unionised white male workers (also see 'dual labour market' theory, p 36).

Activity

Investigate the effects of deskilling on a range of occupations by interviewing relatives and acquaintances.

EVALUATION

Despite the above criticisms, it has to be recognised that Braverman's work is important in adding to our understanding of the changing world of work in a modern society. In the everyday world there are machines that have taken over the skills of former workers. Unemployment, however measured (see p 102 Chapter 8), has continued to rise in most industrial countries from the early 1970s on. There is widespread insecurity about employment among all sections of the working population. Previous secure 'life time' jobs such as banking, law and the civil service are now in the same position of insecurity as any other.

SUMMARY

This chapter has examined the nature of our attitudes to work in an industrial society. At first, issues such as satisfaction at work might appear to be straightforward and somewhat stereotypical in terms of a negative picture of remorseless toil involving repetitive monotonous work with machinery in factories. Clearly Marx saw no possibility of satisfying work for the majority while capitalism continues, but he was optimistic about work satisfaction in a future socialist society. Weber was probably more pessimistic, seeing work in the future as increasingly hidebound in bureaucratic enslavement to rigid rules and regulations which stifle independence of thought and creativity regardless of the type of society. Durkheim was more optimistic about the possibility of the regulation of the division of labour-making work in an 'organic' society more involving and skilled.

The complexity of work satisfaction in our society is such that a fully negative portrait or an overly optimistic one is too simplistic to describe such a complex phenomenon. Braverman has added an important dimension to the debate with his ideas on deskilling evoking continuing debate and argument.

It is probable that satisfaction at work is as varied as the array of jobs that exist, with a lucky few being highly paid in an enjoyable fulfilling job, some finding things sometimes good, sometimes bad, and an unfortunate number working in low paid, low-skilled monotonous drudgery.

Practice questions

1 'Technology determines whether we enjoy our work.' Discuss the contribution made by sociologists in explaining this statement.
2 Examine the view that alienation is the key to understanding work satisfaction.
3 Evaluate Braverman's deskilling thesis.
4 Assess Weber's view that market situation affects the degree of satisfaction to be gained from work.
5 What are the arguments surrounding the idea of an instrumental orientation to work?

Coursework suggestion

Conduct a small survey among your teachers to see what satisfies them and dissatisfies them about their work. Ask how this compares to five or possibly ten years ago (or even further back if older) in order to test the hypothesis above that in the last few years the teaching profession has been affected by political and managerial control undermining their freedom to act in an independent professional manner. Has this lowered levels of job satisfaction?

5

THE CHANGING CONTEXT OF WORK

Introduction

IN THE PREVIOUS chapter the subject of satisfaction with work was examined. It is clear from this that part of the explanation of changes that have occurred concerns how work situations have changed from the beginning of the process of industrialisation. This chapter addresses a number of changes in the context of work which have greatly affected the way we work. One significant change that has previously been discussed concerns the places in which people work.

Table 3: *Concepts, theories, issues and figures in this chapter*			
KEY CONCEPTS	THEORIES	KEY ISSUES	KEY FIGURES
Origins of capitalism	Marxism	Capitalism led to the separation of home from workplace	Engels
Assembly line	Fordism	Assembly lines lead to high productivity and cheaper mass production	Henry Ford
Flexible production	Post-Fordism	Workers need to be flexible and multi-skilled to produce a variety of types and models in a rapidly changing market	Piore and Sabel
McDonaldisation Deskilling Rationalised production	Neo-Weberian	McDonalds style management and working methods is spreading to all workplaces	Ritzer
Bureaucracy	Weberian	Bureaucracy is the most effective form of administration	Max Weber

KEY CONCEPTS	THEORIES	KEY ISSUES	KEY FIGURES
Dysfunction	Neo-Weberian	There are inefficiencies in Bureaucracies	Merton
Mechanistic/organic organisations		Rigid bureaucratic procedures cannot be applied to all organisations	Burns and Stalker
Total Institutions	Interactionist	Stereotypical and often oppositional roles develop in 24-hour institutions such as prisons and mental hospitals	Goffman
Adhocracy		Modern organisations have to be flexible and non-heirarchical	Mintzberg
Postmodern organisations	Postmodernity	Organisations developing teamwork and control from workers	Clegg
		Above more 'democratic' decision making illusory, output still determined from above	Thompson

FROM HOME TO WORKPLACE

THE SEPARATION OF HOME AND WORK

The process of industrialisation accelerated rapidly in the latter part of the nineteenth century and has continued to the present. A key factor in early development was advances in technology which resulted in larger, more productive machines. In the early stages of industrialisation much work was done in the home and the early machinery was small enough to be used there. The case study of the textile industry best illustrates this. Originally weaving of cotton was carried out on hand looms usually kept in the basement. So-called hand loom weavers' cottages are still evident in the original Lancashire cotton towns.

The mid-nineteenth century onward brought significant changes with larger, more efficient textile machinery which, as seen in Chapter 3, had to be housed in separate buildings, the mills and factories we know today. This meant workers had to 'go out' to work, initially not very far as most workers lived in the 'shadow of the mill', within walking and eventually cycling distance.

TEXTILE WORKERS IN THE 19TH CENTURY

Travel to work distances increased as transport developed from the late nineteenth century onward. Such developments physically separated home and workplace and created the idea of 'going out to work', a product of industrialisation. This also created the distinction between the 'public' and the 'private' world in towns and cities. The 'public' world was the workplace and the streets, the 'private' the home and the family. This is today often reflected in social policy where legislation and regulation of the public world is everywhere, but governments and the state are often loath to similarly intervene in the domestic 'private' world of the home and the family. Such issues as the failure to address domestic violence and the smacking of children are sometimes explained by this public/private boundary.

Another issue that arose from the separation of home and workplace concerns the roles of men and women. Engels in *Origin of the Family, Private Property and the State* (1884) saw this as a key aspect of the changed status of men and women, with the former becoming the 'breadwinner' in the public sphere of work, a 'wage slave' of capitalism supported by a housewife and primary childcarer in the private domestic sphere of the home and family. Engels saw this as the root of women's exploitation and oppression in capitalist society. Modern socialist feminists use this analysis to explain women's 'dual burden': today going out to work, but also juggling this with home and childcare with little support from 'breadwinner' men.

Recent developments in technology have led to projections that the home can again become a place of work for increased numbers of people. Computer technology has given rise to a communications revolution which includes the Internet, E-Mail and related developments which will enable people to work from home. It may be that the twenty-first century sees the return of the combined home and workplace for increased numbers, such that the period of human history when the majority went out to work lasted for about 100 years – a relatively short span of time.

Study point

1   What are the implications of such developments as being able to work from home. List some advantages and disadvantages. Will there be advantages to **a** women and **b** the family? Give reasons.
2   Would you prefer to study and eventually work from home? Discuss with your friends, then answer the following in 2–3 paragraphs:

'The growth of homeworking will be of such revolutionary significance in the twenty-first century that within a few years a small minority will go out to work'. Discuss.

MASS PRODUCTION TO FLEXIBLE PRODUCTION

FORDISM: THE ASSEMBLY LINE

The natural thing to do is work – to recognise that prosperity and happiness can be obtained only through honest effort.

Henry Ford

Henry Ford (1863–1947) was the founder of the Ford Motor Company, originally an American car manufacturer. In the early twentieth century, Ford pioneered assembly line mass production of cars, originally in the USA, and eventually in Britain. The original site in Britain was at Trafford Park, Manchester, but it later moved to Dagenham, Essex. Such plants were huge, employing thousands of semi-skilled and unskilled workers who sometimes used bicycles or mechanical trolleys to move from one part of the factory to another.

Ford's first mass production model was the Model T Ford, nicknamed the 'Tin Lizzie' because of its apparent flimsy appearance. What was revolutionary about its assembly line production was its cheaper price compared with other cars.Prior to Ford, cars were built in small craft workshops employing highly skilled tradesmen such as wheelrights and precision engineers. A customer requiring a car would approach such a workshop and specify model and colour, possibly on a Monday, and the car would be ready for him to collect and pay for by Friday of that week. The Model T Ford was around half the price of craft-built cars because of the assembly line which put the division of labour as advocated by Adam Smith (see p 20) and eventually Durkheim (see p 21) into the modern world of mass production of consumer goods. Ford recognised the standardisation and inflexibility that assembly line production involved with his ironic comment on customer choice that, 'You can have any color[sic] you like, so long as it's black.'

Mass production of cars on assembly lines put the majority of traditional craft car building out of business. Enormous profits were made which eventually enabled the Ford Motor Company to expand to its current status as a global empire grossing more annual income than the gross national product of a significant number of the world's developing countries. As discussed in the previous chapter, such production techniques had costs in the loss of job satisfaction. Assembly line work is highlighted as the epitome of boring routine work with little scope for satisfaction in the simple repetitive tasks involved. It is worth noting, however, that the majority of manual factory work is not on assembly lines; assembly line workers are about 10 per cent of manual workers, so it is advisable to avoid generalisation about all workers based on assembly line work only.

POST-FORDISM: THE RETURN TO FLEXIBLE PRODUCTION?

Social scientists such as **Michael Piore** and **C. Sabel** (1984) studying production methods noted changes from the 1970s on. As indicated from the early twentieth century through the post-Second World War period was the heyday of mass production and the assembly line bringing relatively cheap mass consumption goods such as cars,washing machines, fridges and televisions within the reach of the majority of the population, improving average standards of living enormously.

From the 1970s competitiveness had increased such that standardised products were no longer sufficient for an increasingly sophisticated population of consumers who wanted variety and choice in the goods and products they bought. Along with this, the developments in computer technology applied to manufacturing, such as computer-aided design and manufacture (CAD/CAM), led to more flexible production methods which could be altered in a relatively short time. This could give market advantage to companies who applied CAD/CAM to their production.

The type of worker employed in the 'post-Fordist' era is very different to the stereotypical 'instrumental' assembly line worker. The newer worker needs to be adaptable and flexible in their approach to work as the environment is regularly changing. An advantage is that work has potentially become more variable and interesting, counteracting the drudgery of previous forms of work. Workers are encouraged to work in teams, organising how they go about tasks between them, rather than have old style 'external' supervision from foremen/women and managers. A well-known example of this is Volvo cars in Sweden who in the 1970s scrapped their assembly lines and built new factories to encourage 'team' production methods. Each team included a range of skilled workers who were charged with taking a car from the beginning to the end of production. They could carry out tasks in their own way as decided within the team. Volvo saw clear advantages to this compared with the assembly line where absenteeism, sickness and high labour turnover were seriously affecting production. The new work methods were seen to bring elements of creativity, involvement and pride into car production. Workers saw the car from initial stages to completed production, giving them a sense of identity with their labour which was very different to the assembly line worker doing one small task repetitively where there was no sense of a completed product. The evidence from such an 'experiment' is somewhat mixed; there was not the hoped for improvements in productivity, but worker satisfaction had improved with lower rates of absenteeism, sickness and labour turnover.

Activity
Write a short passage comparing and contrasting the deskilling debate in the previous chapter with the 'post-Fordist' position above. Which is most optimistic and which most pessimistic about the development of work. Give reasons.

The idea of a post-Fordist industry has similarity to some of the key ideas in postmodernism and the post-industrialism debate considered in other sections of this book (see pp 63 and 137).

MCDONALDIZATION

Some points of criticism concerning the view that we live in a world of post-Fordist work were raised above. While it is true that certain industries have followed such a path there still remain thousands of manual workers who are in monotonous factory jobs. Following on from the deskilling debate and issues raised by feminist sociologists, there are similarly thousands of white collar non-manual workers who are in clerical and administrative jobs where work is every bit as routine and unfulfilling as the most boring factory work.

Braverman (see p 44) saw deskilling spreading throughout the labour force as the capitalist system used technology such as mechanisation and automation to replace potentially powerful craft and skilled workers. **George Ritzer** (1993) takes this a stage further in *The McDonaldization of Society*. He applies the Weberian concept of rationality to the way modern workplaces have developed. Since the 1980s there has been a dramatic increase in the production of fast food, such that outlets have now come to dominate every high street, shopping mall, sports and leisure complex. Ritzer chose one of the most successful and well-known as an 'ideal type' (a Weberian concept originally applied to bureaucracy). McDonalds is American-owned and is now a global corporation having outlets in virtually every major city in the world, such that the price of a 'BigMac' is used by economists as an indicator of a country's standard of living. The success of McDonalds came from the application of rationalised mass production techniques to the manufacture of fast food. Most of McDonalds food is prepared in centralised factories where mechanisation and automation is used wherever possible to create a standard product. This means that outlets can employ unskilled and easily trainable staff on part-time and temporary contracts to do the fairly simple finishing tasks to the food to be served to customers. Everything is measured and quantified by machinery even to the amount of relish on a burger and the number of 'French Fries' per portion. Spot checks are made by area inspectors posing as customers, and workers can be disciplined for serving too large portions or not interacting with customers in the standard approved manner. The workforce are all part-time, often students and younger people, who are paid above the usual rates for part-time unskilled work. Another feature of the work is a strong emphasis on American-style 'customer care' where workers are given 'scripts' indicating what to say and how to interact with customers. So such instructions as smiling and greeting 'Enjoy your meal' plus admonitions to spend more 'Would you like extra fries/a large Coke?' are part of the training programme. Successful completion of such programmes brings symbols of merit such as star lapel badges. Increases in sales and productivity are encouraged by monthly prize trips to leisure parks and clubs for selected teams or 'crew members'.

Some fast food companies have tried to introduce shift or day contracts which mean that workers are only paid if customers are present. A Burger King restaurant in Glasgow attracted media attention in the early 1990s when it was reported that workers had received £1 after completing a four-hour shift. Such practices caused outrage and have been curtailed by legislation and the introduction of an hourly minimum wage of £3.60 in 1999. It can be noted, however, that such legislation applies mainly to 21 year olds and over, with younger workers of the type usually employed by fast food companies receiving less employment protection.

Ritzer moves beyond fast food production to argue that there has been a 'McDonaldization' of society. Quantified fast food production methods, American-style management and employee behaviour requirements can now be seen in all types of work situation, ranging from pubs to travel companies, from teaching to social work. Concepts such as Total Quality Management (TQM) have been borrowed from American managerial gurus such as **Tom Peters** and applied to companies stressing 'quality', 'performance indicators' and 'customer care' with evangelical zeal.

The benefits of such a customer-focused approach where formerly patients, students and school pupils become 'clients', 'consumers' or 'stakeholders' have been emphasised. Such trends are seen as healthy and democratic, 'empowering' workers, and putting customers needs and their rights to 'quality' and 'good service' to the fore, making for a successful future for the organisation.

Critics such as Ritzer have pointed to a darker side of this world as creating a robotised 'iron cage' for low-paid workers who are easily expendable in competitive business climates and made to shoulder the blame for business failure.

The 'McDonaldization of Society' is a powerful idea to be considered along with 'deskilling' and compared to the arguments of 'post-Fordists'. Perhaps each position can be accused of over-generalisation to a complex world where all aspects of the three positions can be found in elements of the labour force. Another element is that all three imply such forces as being irresistible when in fact worker rejection and resistance can make the picture more complex. Artificial friendliness such as 'Have a nice day' become meaningless mantras displayed through gritted teeth.

On closer examination, concepts such as 'quality' and 'performance indicators' become very difficult to pin down and convey to workers. Some industries have found that improvements from the implementation of TQM in organisations has been short-lived with initial enthusiasm reducing with a return to previous working styles.

Marxists criticise such developments suggesting all are in the interests of capitalism. The capitalist continues to seek ways to pay workers as little as possible with improved productivity under the guise of worker involvement and 'empowerment'. This results in individual and 'team' blame for business failure rather than the economic system itself.

Activity
You may work/have worked in a job such as above. If not, find someone who has and discuss the picture of work portrayed. Indicate strengths and weaknesses to judge how accurate or truthful such accounts are.

THE BUREAUCRACY DEBATE

GROWTH IN SIZE AND SCALE OF ORGANISATIONS

A key feature of the development of industrial societies through the twentieth century has been the growth in scale and size of the workplace. In the early stages of industrialisation, firms were small and relationships between workers were close-knit and personal. As cited previously, the owners or capitalists were closely involved with the day-to-day affairs of their company, often walking around and talking to individual workers. This gradually changed as firms merged and increased their scale of operations, such that firms originally employing up to 50 workers became national and eventually international companies, employing thousands of workers. This resulted in a loss of personal contact and identity with owners and other workers outside the immediate 'shop' or area of work.

THE CONTRIBUTION OF WEBER

This growth in scale and size and the requirement for complex forms of administration was a feature of developing industrialisation recognised by Weber from the late nineteenth century on. Weber highlighted the growth of bureaucracy (literally rule by the office), a particular form of administration that he regarded as the most efficient for carrying out such tasks. He likened bureaucracy to a machine with the parts interconnecting toward the whole to carry out a particular task efficiently. He saw the division of labour in factory production as being replicated in a bureaucracy. Instead of material products bureaucracy produces effective administration:

the decisive reason for the advance of bureaucratic organisation has always been its purely technical supremacy over other forms of organisation. The fully developed bureaucratic mechanism compares with other organisations exactly as does the machine with non-mechanical modes of production.

From Max Weber, Routledge & Kegan Paul, London 1948 (Hans H. Gerth and C. Wright Mills, 1948) (eds.)

There is a heirarchy of officials whose authority is unquestioningly accepted; this type of authority Weber termed 'Legal-Rational', where power was invested in that particular position or role.

This compared with other forms of authority:

- 'Traditional' where control is handed down through the generations as in the case of father handing over to son;
- 'Charismatic' where control comes from the personal qualities and attributes of a particular individual leader (sometimes described as their 'aura') as in the leader of a religious sect.

It is worth noting that Weber used the term 'Ideal Type' bureaucracy to convey that his model did not apply to all bureaucracies and their variations but highlighted common features, just as an 'Ideal Type' horse does not cover variations in, eg, colour (brown, black, white), size (large, small), breed (Arabian, Shetland) and function (racehorse, carthorse).

The following are the key features of bureaucracy as identified by Weber:

- officials chosen solely according to their ability with impersonal authority;
- tasks or duties carried out only according to a specific set of rules and regulations which are inflexible and cannot be changed – today referred to as 'red tape' from the red ribbon that used to bind French Civil Service documents;
- such rules and regulations are written down and to be consulted for instruction on how to act in particular circumstances;
- a chain of command or heirarchy where officials above control those below.

Weber recognised the negative dimensions of this 'faceless' type of official and inflexible organisation trapped in an 'iron cage'. However he saw the trend to bureaucratisation as inevitable if efficient administration was required as other forms of organisation and associated authority were more inefficient and less democratic. For example, in a traditional authority organisation the boss's son might be incompetent, or a charismatic leader might turn into a raving demagogue as has happened in the cases of mass suicide in some religious sects.

CRITICISMS OF WEBER

Modern writers on bureaucracy have taken issue with a number of aspects of Weber's approach. Despite some negativity he stressed the efficiency of such an organisation which does not accord with the modern experience. Today 'bureaucracy' or 'bureaucrat' has acquired negative connotations associated with inefficiency and insensitivity particularly in those dealing with the public, such as Social Security offices. Weber did not really address issues arising from public service bureaucracies where bureaucratic needs and adherence to procedures, resulting in impersonality and rigidity in rule following, hinders the aim of the organisation, ie service to the public.

Study point

Have you had any dealings with bureaucracy? If not ask friends/relatives and make a note of experience of inefficiency as suggested above.

DYSFUNCTIONS OF BUREAUCRACY

Some sociologists such as **Robert Merton** (1968) have noted such negative tendencies and described them as 'dysfunctions of bureaucracy', where as well as inflexibility, the size and scale hinder efficiency and effective communication. This is reflected in mass media portrayals where accounts of 'bungling town hall bureaucrats' are regularly featured.

Some sociologists have recognised this and have devised models to accommodate this modern complexity. A well-known one is that of **Tom Burns** and **G.M. Stalker** (1961) who used the typology of mechanistic and organic organisations:

* Mechanistic – this is similar to Weber's 'Ideal Type' bureaucracy where there are clearly defined rules and a heirarchy of officials each with a clear proscribed role;
* Organic organisations are more flexible and able to cope with change more effectively. A lessening of rigid heirarchies and the encouragement of innovation and change from all staff has shifted the focus from management and direction from above to flatter team-based decision-making more appropriate to a modern world of business and industry in a volatile and competitive market situation.

Alvin W. Gouldner (1954), in a study of a gypsum mine in America, found that as well as a need for coping with change, the actual task or purpose of the organisation can dictate how bureaucratic or mechanistic they are. He found that the mine offices and administrative sections above the ground tended to be of the mechanistic or bureaucratic type operating in a fairly stable environment where rigid rules and procedures could be followed. Such conditions did not apply below ground in the mine itself where the work was physically demanding, dangerous and subject to sudden problems such as subsidence or seam collapse. Here much more flexibility had to be allowed for such circumstances as often split-second decisions had to be made by individuals or teams. So an organic form of organisational structure had evolved to accommodate such circumstances.

FORMAL AND INFORMAL ORGANISATIONS

From the 1960s interpretive sociologists studying various types of organisations pointed to the importance of interaction within organisations between members and groups. This highlighted how important the hidden or 'informal' aspects of behaviour in such organisations were. An organisation might be formally presented as a smooth running machine by managers and higher officials but in fact 'behind the scenes' things operate differently.

Erving Goffman (1968) carried out a participant observational study of a mental hospital in America. The term he used for such '24-hour involvement' organisations which covered boarding schools, military camps, monasteries and ships at sea was '**Total Institutions**'. He found a 'staff-inmate' divide with each side stereotyping the other. He applied his earlier idea of everyday life as a sort of stage with social actors who perform particular roles according to a 'script'. For patients the 'script' dictates a range of appropriate roles which they act out, and similarly for staff, who can be kind, caring, or therapeutic on the one hand or punitive and cruel on the other. This world is very different to that presented by directors on 'Open Days' or visits.

Study point

When you next attend such a formal event as a prize-giving or 'speech day' at a school or college note the image of the institution presented by the Head or Principal and compare it to the everyday reality for students and staff.

In prisons it is well known that staff allow the prisoners significant leeway in their behaviour to enable the prison to remain fairly stable. So unofficial rule-breaking or more serious activities such as drug-taking are recognised but often ignored for the sake of maintaining peace and harmony in a stressful environment where over-disciplinarian approaches can result in riots and other costly outcomes as many prisoners 'have nothing to lose'. Sometimes rule-breaking can be sanctioned at a higher level as when it was advocated as a policy that free condoms should be issued to prisoners to encourage safe sexual practices.

Study point

1   Take any two of the above and show how informal interactions can operate in similar ways to mental hospitals and prisons.
2   Which of the following are:
    a mechanistic bureaucracies **b** organic organisations or **c** total institutions:
    A school; a university; the civil service; a hospital; the Army; an advertising agency; a coal mine; a drug rehabilitation centre.

Give reasons and explain why some might be difficult to place.

At the theoretical level, apart from interpretivists such as Goffman who carry out small scale studies, other structuralist sociologists such as Salaman in *Class and the Corporation* (1979) have analysed organisations in Marxist terms, presenting a class conflict approach and emphasising the role of bureaucracies and similar organisations in preserving capitalist interests. One example would be the way social security departments and social work agencies do not in fact serve the interests of the poor and deprived but encourage them to put up with their poverty by explaining things in terms of rigid inflexible rules, 'That's the way it is'. This discourages action and criticism and rewards the subservient 'client' who is content with his or her 'lot'.

A combination of interpretive and conflict perspectives was displayed in the 1970s film based on the novel *One Flew Over the Cuckoo's Nest*, set in the ward of a mental hospital. A rebellious newcomer, McMurphy played by Jack Nicholson, threatens to upset the smooth-running sedative-based regime run by the tyrannical Nurse Ratchett. As he gradually becomes more dominant and causes even the most compliant patients to rebel, Nurse Ratchett realises he must be quashed. At first electro-convulsive therapy is used with partial success but McMurphy recovers and the film ends after he receives a personality-destroying lobotomy and is suffocated by another patient who sees the institution as having already killed McMurphy and thus thwarting the 'rebellion'. This patient himself escapes in the closing scene.

How would a conflict theorist explain this film?

Henry Mintzberg (1983) identifies a number of types of organisation ranging from the simple small organisation through conventional bureaucracies, to the 'adhocracy'. This latter more modern form of organisation best accords with some of the key aspects of a post-Fordist industry. An adhocracy organisation is flexible and non-heirarchical. It is constantly adapting to change and volatile market and business conditions. Personnel work in multi-disciplinary teams which focus on 'projects' which when completed may result in people leaving to join other teams. Unlike Weber's 'ideal type' bureaucracy each member of a team is seen as having equal worth and status.This type of responsive and adaptable organisation avoids the negative aspects of bureaucracy such as slow response and impersonality. Mintzberg sees the adhocracy as the organisational structure of the future.

Study point

Summarise some of the key features of an adhocracy and show how there are links to post-Fordism and postmodern forms of organisation (see below).

Modern and Postmodern Organisations

Stuart Clegg (1992) sees the decline of traditional large manufacturing companies in a rapidly changing world as a factor in the undermining of the need for bureaucratic organisations. Such companies were based on a recognisable division of labour with a heirarchy based on specialised tasks. Such differentiated tasks have now been replaced by a process of what Clegg refers to as 'de-differentiation' which involves jobs being less specialised and work roles becoming more diverse. An example of this is the changes in the 1970s Volvo plant previously referred to (see p 55) where teams of workers cooperated and jointly built a car from the raw material to the completed stage. Within the team there were specialists but they could decide to do other tasks thus rotating the division of labour and making work more involving and interesting. Clegg sees Japanese companies as epitomising trends toward postmodern organisations. There is an emphasis on teamwork and decision-making within the team. A team usually has a pre-work meeting to discuss the previous day's work and decide how to go about the day's tasks. Quality circles self-monitor progress and standards and are encouraged to innovate. Unlike conventional bureaucracies, external authority is played down in favour of the encouragement of company or corporate loyalty. The undermining of heirarchy is seen in work clothing where senior officials wear the same company uniform (overalls, baseball cap) as everyone else. An interesting feature of Japanese companies establishing plants and factories in Britain was their changing of old symbols of status and heirarchy, such as separate canteen and restaurant for workers and managers being replaced by communal dining areas where managers queued for self-service along with the rest of the workforce. The benefits of such 'postmodern' approaches are seen in terms of developing corporate culture and strong company loyalties.

This 'postmodern' style has had an effect on many companies in Britain and has encroached into public services such as education. In schools and colleges there is now an emphasis on 'corporate identity' where students and staff are encouraged to take pride in belonging to that organisation. Similarly in the health service, hospitals have also evolved 'corporate identities'. In such settings workers of all levels belong to teams and work in ways which reinforce this.

SUMMARY

This chapter has looked at the changing context of work from a range of angles. Earlier perspectives concerning the change from pre-industrial to industrial society emphasised a number of changes such as 'going out to work' as well as the shift to factory production, resulting in effects on homes and families and relationships between men and women.

Part of this was associated with the growth in scale and size of technology which led to the development of large factories which needed more complex forms of organisation and administration. In the late nineteenth and early twentieth centuries Weber saw the most efficient form of administration to be bureaucracy. Modern sociologists studying organisations have questioned this, highlighting the negative features of impersonality and inefficiency, particularly in those providing a public service. Another factor is that many modern organisations need to be flexible and adaptable to a rapidly changing world. Conventional bureaucratic structures would hamper this. Some commentators such as Clegg and Mintzberg have seen the future in terms of 'postmodern' or 'adhocratic' organisations where conventional heirarchical structures have been broken down into non-specialised teamwork involved in short term 'projects'. Others question this, seeing such developments as limited to a few industries that need to respond rapidly to dynamic technological and business changes. Even within such 'chaos' companies, there still remain controls and demands from higher levels of management pressing for increased productivity and seeking profits in ways that would still be recognised by Karl Marx.

Ritzer provides another perspective following on from the deskilling debate. He combines this with a neo-Weberian view on the growth of rationalised production. His 'McDonaldization' thesis is that the American fast food company with its highly organised rational production methods for fast food has provided a model for a range of modern companies. The employment of low-skilled, part-time, short-term contractual workers who are easily replaced and trained in 'customer-focused' service and an emphasis on corporate culture and teamwork within 'crews' has spread to many work organisations. Hospitals, airlines, colleges, and public services have now become 'client' or 'customer' focused with proud displays of 'quality' improvement and customer charters. At first this may seem like good thing – a sign of a more democratic and less bureaucratic organisation in the future. But behind the enforced smile and commitment to service are highly pressurised and insecure workers who are controlled and managed in more effective ways than in former times.

Clearly the development of industrialisation has led to changes in the context of work. In modern socities many now 'go out' to work in large bureaucratic organisations. Postmodern developments may be changing this for some workers. Communications and technological developments mean that more of us will be able to work at home than at present, which could possibly liberate formerly restricted and discriminated against groups such as women, ethnic minorities and the disabled. This may seem a positive development for the future but when accompanied by low pay, short-term contracts and associated insecurities, the future for workers in organisations looks less bright.

STUDY GUIDE

Practice questions

1 'Bureaucracy is the most effective form of administration' Discuss
2 Why does Ritzer advocate the 'McDonaldization of Society'?
3 'Postmodern organisations have unpredictable,non-heirarchical structures where workers have more control and power over what they do.' Discuss

---

Coursework suggestions

1 Conduct a survey on attitudes to bureaucracy. Investigate whether people feel positive or negative and what their experience is. You need to consider ways to operationalise bureaucracy, ie. discuss it in a comprehensible form, perhaps focusing on the town hall or government departments such as tax offices.
2 If you can find a small group who work in McDonalds or similar workplaces you can use them as a case study to investigate the key elements of Ritzer's ideas. Compare with other jobs to see if 'McDonaldization' is widespread.

6

INEQUALITY IN THE WORKPLACE

Introduction

THIS CHAPTER EXAMINES social divisions and inequality at work. The traditional sociological approach was to examine social class as occupation and one's position in the economic system related to where one stood in society. The classic divide was between manual and non-manual work with the former being seen as working class and the latter as middle. Such divisions were probably more clear cut and recognisable in the past, with manual workers engaged in dirty and demanding physical work and non-manual workers engaged in sedentary office-type work involving using the mind in some capacity or another; hence the adage 'brains or brawn' applied to this distinction. With technological advances leading to increased mechanisation and automation, such a division became less clear with machines taking over much heavy physical work and the 'deskilling' of many office and clerical tasks making them as routine, boring and mindless as any manual job.

Another factor was the enormous increase in women workers. In the past adult women on marriage often gave up work, in some occupations such as the civil service and teaching it was compulsory to do so until the late 1940s. In the working classes, with some exceptions such as in textile areas it was assumed that marriage meant being a housewife and mother. For a man it was important that his working wage could support a wife and family; a view of a 'family wage' that continued in union negotiations on pay until relatively recently. Up to the mid-twentieth century, when sociologists discussed inequality and the stratification of society their prime focus was on social class. From the 1960s on, the impact of feminism highlighted gender as another social division to be considered, for some replacing social class as the key inequality, for others to be considered along with social class. Later, other elements of the division of society such as ethnicity, age, disability and sexuality were also seen as important dimensions in explaining inequality between people in society.

Table 5: *Concepts, theories, issues and figures in this chapter*			
KEY CONCEPTS	THEORIES	KEY ISSUES	KEY FIGURES
Class	Marxism	Work is divided on class lines	Marx
Manual/Non-manual			
Conditions and pay			
Gender inequality	Feminism	Men have more power and control in the workplace	
		Women working full-time do more domestic work than partners	Elston
		Women in socialist societies not equal with men	Lane Scott
Job segregation		Women in different jobs or in lower positions if same area of work	Hartmann
Women's 'choice'	Post-feminism	Women's full-time equivalent work hours have not changed, indicating their 'choice' to stay at home	Hakim Breugel Crompton
Ethnicity	Neo-Marxist	Discrimination and prejudice against ethnic groups can be explained in terms of class conflict	Castles and Kosack
	Neo-Weberian	Subjective aspects of prejudice based on skin colour rooted in culture and history	Rex and Tomlinson
Age heirarchy		Older workers skills no longer necessary	Mead
Disability	Labelling	Disabled stigmatised and denied access to able-bodied society	Shakespeare

SOCIAL CLASS IN THE WORKPLACE

MARXIST APPROACHES

For Marxists social class is the key to explaining all aspects of inequality whether it affects women in relation to men, black and Asian people in relation to white, the old compared with the young,the disabled compared with the able-bodied, or the gay compared with the heterosexual. You have already encountered the Marxist model of the class structure under capitalism which broadly suggests two major classes based on ownership (Bourgeoisie/Capitalist) or non-ownership (Proletariat/Working Class) of the means of production. The relationship between the two is exploitative and a cause of conflict, such that Marx predicted the eventual downfall of capitalism. All other divisions in society centre around this. For example, racism between workers is caused by class inequalities. Divisions among the working class on ethnic grounds with whites discriminating against blacks and Asians, has the effect of 'divide and rule'. If the pay of white people is poor and employment is threatened, they blame 'immigrants' or black people for taking 'our jobs', a message enthusiastically fuelled by racist political groups. For Marxists this works to support capitalist interests as attention is diverted from the real cause of low pay and unemployment which is the capitalist system with its greedy pursuit of maximum profits for the minority ruling or capitalist class. Another dimension is that vulnerable workers such as unskilled immigrants have to accept any job and low pay so can be used as a 'Reserve Army of Labour' to keep all pay levels down.

Marxist approaches to other inequalities will be explained in the sections below.

MANUAL AND NON-MANUAL WORK

Until the mid-twentieth century, work was commonly divided into manual and non-manual categories and this was used to distinguish the working class from the middle class in a number of typologies of class, such as the Registrar-General's Index used in the ten-yearly census of the UK population, a government survey. Up to that time most jobs could be identified in terms of either physical labour using strength to carry out work tasks, or in terms of mental labour using the brain or mind to carry out work tasks.

As industrialisation developed, further complexities arose, some associated with mechanisation and automation. Technological developments began to replace manual labour in such tasks as lifting (cranes and fork lift trucks). Driving such machinery was still described as manual work. Process workers in automated chemical plants who observed dials, gauges and instruments to monitor production often dressed in white overalls, keeping as clean as any office worker.

The growth of the service and distributive sector has led to thousands of jobs in banking, catering, hotels, travel and tourism, insurance, shops and supermarkets. The low-grade jobs in this sector offer the lowest rates of pay of any occupation and are often part time. Another dimension is that much of the lower-grade work is carried out by women (see below). A more recent complication in determining manual/non-manual distinctions at work is the computer which has meant a whole range of related jobs which do not neatly fit into such a division.

However, when it comes to earnings, some aspect of a manual/non-manual divide is evident. With few exceptions the majority of the highest earners (£100,000+) are in non-manual middle-class occupations. Many of the lowest earners are in manual occupations such as labouring. However, as the previous paragraph suggested there are a significant number of low-paid, lower white collar workers such as shop assistants and hotel workers who are the bottom of any earnings league. The added dimension is that many of them are women.

From the above, it can be seen why the changed nature of work in modern societies has led many to suggest that we are in some way 'classless' to the extent that there are now no clear boundaries between the classes. Such a view is sometimes espoused by politicians but critics from a Marxist perspective point out that it is to be expected from those who want to preserve the *status quo* and vindicate their policies in creating a supposedly more prosperous unified society.

A further dimension of class differences in pay is that in general the middle classes receive annual increments to their salary which are provided automatically. Traditionally, a typical middle-class career trajectory involves gradually increasing pay from relatively low in the 20s to high levels in the 50s and 60s. A working-class occupation does not usually involve annual increments; if an apprenticeship is served, once completed the full adult rate is paid and this can remain the same except for inflationary pay increases until retirement. Another element is that older workers can receive lower pay, as pay is often based on speed and physical strength which diminishes with age. So a young bricklayer can earn top money because he lays thousands of bricks per day. Older bricklayers cannot work as fast so are paid less. The differences are portrayed in the following graphs.

As well as pay increments, middle-class careers involve promotion to higher pay scales which further adds to class inequalities. So comparing pay between two young workers needs to take such life course differences into account.

Traditionally Retirement Pensions were calculated on the amount earned in the last 3 years of employment. How would this favour the middle class worker?

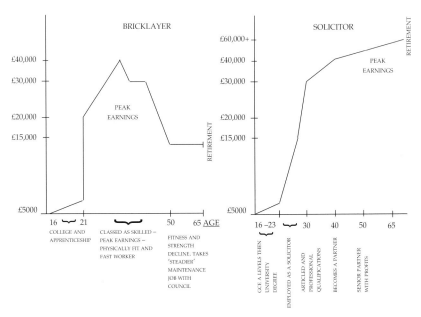

TWO GRAPHS COMPARING LIFETIME EARNINGS OF MANUAL AND A PROFESSIONAL WORKER

Consider the following case studies:

Andrew is a 22-year-old bricklayer. He is good at his job, and on a large housebuilding site earns in excess of £500 per week (approximately £25,000 a year).

Alex is a trainee solicitor. At 22, she has recently graduated from university and is now employed in a large law firm on an annual salary of £18,000 a year.

- In the light of the previous section show how Andrew and Alex's careers may progress until retirement.
- Do the differences in salary show that middle- and working-class differences in pay are no longer relevant in arguments about class inequality?

The above scenario of middle/working class pay/salary differentials may seem to be overdrawn in the light of recent volatility in the labour market. Middle-class occupations are now more insecure, so a smooth lifetime career trajectory from relatively low earnings to high salaries involving promotions and seniority is becoming less available. Redundancy and greater insecurity offering reduced income from age 50 on has been an experience that has affected an increasing number of the middle-class from the 1980s.

However, despite this, it is still a general feature of the professions that the majority can expect a lifetime career with accompanying promotion and high salaries. How long this will continue is a matter for speculation (see Chapter 10).

CONDITIONS OF WORK

As well as earnings, jobs involve particular conditions. Here it seems clear that the dirtiest, noisiest, most uncomfortable and dangerous work is in manual occupations. There is probably nothing comparable in any non-manual job to the conditions of a miner flat on their stomach in a narrow coal seam in temperatures of 100 degrees or a diver working on the construction of an oil platform several hundred feet below water in dark conditions, lit by floodlights. Such examples

DIFFERENT WORKING CONDITIONS: COAL MINERS AND AN OFFICE WORKER

may seem exceptional, but there are many more familiar everyday jobs which offer discomfort and difficult conditions. Everyday observation of labourers on building sites or digging holes in the road and garage mechanics shows that many manual jobs involve dirt and discomfort with sometimes attendant dangers. Even bodily functions have to be carried out in semi-public. Compare this with the situation of non-manual workers working in comfortable centrally heated or air-conditioned offices with drinks machines available, comfortable chairs and desks and a communal 'relaxation' area.

FRINGE BENEFITS

Another dimension of the conditions of work is fringe benefits, sometimes referred to as 'perks', which are most in evidence in middle-class occupations. 'Fringe benefits' are extras to a salary and can include company cars, subsidised restaurants, free hairstyling, pensions, private medical treatment and help with school fees. Some of the more lucrative of these, which can include a house and its maintenance, are only available to the most senior ranks of the middle class.

So fringe benefits apply much more to middle-class occupations than those of the working class, an extra dimension to the inequalities of social class.

SUMMARY

There have been some changes in the work situation that have meant that in certain areas boundaries and class differences have become blurred as in the enormous growth in insecure, low-paid, part-time 'white collar' work in the service and distributive industries. However despite this, arguments about 'classlessness' applied to the whole of work cannot be fully generalised. Closer examination shows fairly clear evidence that differences remain from the more concrete, in the higher salaries of most middle-class occupations, to the more abstract, with the differences in benefits such as comfortable conditions and fringe benefits. Postmodern accounts may point to the inevitable blurring of such barriers as volatility, unpredictability and insecurity impact on all of us. But it still seems that for the near future class differences in the work situation remain.

GENDER INEQUALITIES AT WORK

If I want to create employment, should I target full-time men who are on the dole and may never get a job or should I encourage low-paid part-time employment for mostly middle-class women?'

Deputy Prime Minister John Prescott, speech 1994

Activity

1 'The lawyer has a brother who goes to sea. The brother who goes to sea has not got a brother'. Explain.
2 A surgeon is tragically killed in a car accident. His accompanying son is seriously injured. On entering the operating theatre the shocked surgeon gasped, 'I cannot operate, that is my son!' Explain.

(see p 91 for discussion of the above and a coursework suggestion.)

Debates about inequality surrounding social class have dominated Sociology since its origins in the nineteenth century. From the 1960s another significant dimension of inequality was increasingly highlighted by feminist scholars. This concerns the differences in opportunities between men and women in all walks of life including work. You should now be familiar with how this has been explained through feminist theories ranging from:

- Liberal feminists who are optimistic about change and the increase in opportunities for women. They would point to education where girls have overtaken boys in qualifications such as GCSEs and A-Levels as a portent for the future. There are now more female solicitors under 30 years than male and half of current medical students are women. Liberal feminists are reformists who see the possibility of change in the existing system, for example by political activity to change discriminatory laws.

- Marxist or socialist feminists see such changes as superficial because key aspects of structural inequality are overlooked by liberal feminists. They see the root cause of women's oppression as the capitalist system. Women are still concentrated in low-paid exploitative conditions in ways which Marxists describe as a 'Reserve Army of Labour' (see p 19). Their domestic and family commitments are part of the explanation of this. Even women in the professions experience inequality. When they have children, female doctors have to work less hours than their male counterparts. Consequently their careers and promotion opportunities are more restricted. **M. Elston's** (1980) study of full-time doctors married to other doctors showed that the wife still carried out over 80 per cent of the housework in her time outside working hours. Also within the family ideological aspects of the capitalist system are reproduced, for example a mother's busy 'juggling' dual role of home and work are conveyed to children as 'natural' for women.

- Radical feminists dispute the role of capitalism as the source of gender inequality. They point to male/female inequality in all types of society, whether communist or capitalist. For example studies of the USSR and Czechoslovakia in the 1970s by **David Lane** (1970) and **Hilda Scott** (1976) in once communist and socialist societies showed that although women participated in the labour force more equally they still were the prime childcarers and houseworkers with men having little or no involvement. Some argued that women's position was, if anything, worse than in a capitalist society. This was because the early socialist societies eschewed any service industries such as corner shops, laundries and bakeries as these were seen ideologically as vestiges of capitalist enterprises. Ironically, it is such services as these which have helped women in western societies participate more equally in the labour market with men. There is some evidence that participating in full-time labour as well as home and family is creating a burden of stress on women in such societies as indicated by reports that mental ill-health and stress-related illnesses have increased dramatically in recent years. Radical feminists see patriarchy as the root cause of women's unequal position in all societies.

Women's subordinate position at work has been explained by 'dual labour market' theory (see p 36) where women tend to be more often employed in the secondary market; and by the Marxist 'reserve army of labour' where women are part of the expendable and easily exploitable groups at the bottom end of the labour market.

Feminists such as **Heidi Hartmann** (1982) have explained the labour market in terms gender-based job segregation. Segregation can be horizontal or vertical.

Horizontal Segregation

This is where men and women are in different types of work such as male managers and doctors and female secretaries and nurses. It could be argued that this should now start to change as the effect of increasing numbers of more highly qualified females leaving schools and colleges makes an impact on such segregation. This is backed by Equal Opportunities legislation, originally passed in 1975, which has helped to create a climate where discrimination against women is unacceptable. An increasing number of previously stereotypical male occupations, such as management, are being taken up by women, helping to undermine previous assumptions about 'men's work' and 'women's work'.

Study point

Is it that easy to alter perceptions of 'men's' and 'women's' work? Suggest some barriers that women may face in occupying formerly male positions such as lorry driving and the legal profession.

Vertical Segregation

This is where women and men are in similar occupations and professions but women tend to be in the subordinate or less glamorous low-paid areas and men in the more senior highly paid areas. It has already been noted that among factory workers, it is men who tend to be operating machines and involved with technology while women are in the more unskilled low-paid routine jobs such as assembling electronic components at a bench.

In medicine the less 'glamorous' (equals lower paid) specialisms such as paediatrics and geriatrics tend to be proportionately more female, whereas brain and heart surgery offering the highest salaries and accompanying prestige is almost wholly male. It will be insteresting to observe if, in the future with increased numbers of women currently studying medicine, the so-called 'glamorous' specialisms become less so. There are two historical examples of this.In the late nineteenth century most clerical workers in the civil service were men and such positions were given prestige in terms of 'respectable pillars of the community' in secure salaried employment. Early in the twentieth century a significant number of boys' schools taught typing and secretarial subjects as town halls and offices mainly employed men. By the mid-twentieth century this had reversed, such that secretarial and office work became female. Such work is seen differently now in terms of lower status and prestige than when it was almost exclusively male. In the Soviet Union in the 1960s it was thought that the almost equal number of male and female lawyers was a sign of socialist 'emancipation' until it was realised that legal work had much lower status than in the west, so what appeared as an 'advance' was not in fact so.

This argument that the 'feminisation' of occupations leads to lowered pay and status has recently been used in reverse when it was advocated by their trades unions and professional associations that nursing and primary school teaching should aim to attract more men thus raising the profile of such professions enhancing pay, conditions and status.

THE CONTROVERSY OVER WOMEN'S 'CHOICE' AND HOURS OF WORK

Hakim's myths

In 1995 Dr **Catherine Hakim**, a Senior Research Fellow at the prestigious London School of Economics raised a storm of protest among fellow feminist academics when the *British Journal of Sociology* published her article, 'Five Feminist Myths about Women's Employment'.

The 'myths' are as follows:

1 Women's employment has been rising
2 Women's work orientation/commitment is equal to men's
3 (Lack of) childcare is the main barrier to women's employment

4   Part-timers are exploited in poor quality jobs
5   Women's stability of employment is equal to men's .

The basis for her argument that each of the above are 'myths' is a statistical analysis of the volume of female employment in the post-Second World War decades. Most correctly assume that the numbers of women in the workforce has increased, but Hakim points out that when measured in full-time equivalent numbers there has been no increase in the volume of female employment. Another way of putting this is to point to the increase in numbers of part- time women workers as the result of the substitution of part-time for full-time jobs. This of course has affected male workers also, but proportionately a far greater number of women are involved.

The controversial dimension of Hakim's argument is that a key reason for the lack of increase in full-time equivalent hours is women's choice not to take up working opportunities on an equal basis to men. This contradicts conventional feminist arguments that emphasise the restricted and exploitative opportunities available to women in a patriarchical society. Men are in power in most workplaces and in the family childcare is automatically taken as a woman's responsibility.

Study point

From your own knowledge and experience, which of the two positions above seem most correct? Ask female friends and relatives about their experiences of work and childcare to examine elements of choice or restriction in women's opportunities compared to men.

Hakim also points to the increase in opportunities for women reinforced by 1970s legislation on equal pay and opportunities. Many employers now like to publicise such aspects of their organisation and can operate informal positive discrimination in favour of women candidates. There is continual media publicity about women in 'top' jobs, and there are campaigns to encourage females to take up previously male occupations, such as the early 1990s 'Women into Science and Engineering' (WISE) promotion.

This shift in attitudes has been around since the 1970s, but according to Hakim has not been reflected in an increase in women's full-time commitment to work.

Hakim on Choice
In another work Hakim (1996) identifies three types of women whose 'choices' are played out differently:

1 the **career woman** who has high commitment to employment and invests heavily in educational qualifications
2 the **homemaker** who is less committed to employment putting home and family first
3 the **drifter** who has a chaotically unplanned employment career.

This view is summarised effectively in the following extract:

> *Women are responsible adults,who make real choices and are the authors and agents of their own lives. Some women choose to be home-centred, with work as a secondary activity. Some women choose to be career-centred, with domestic activities a secondary consideration. Female heterogeneity is a result of the choices women make, reflecting not just different but conflicting preferences between two qualitatively different life courses.*
>
> Catherine Hakim, *Key Issues in Women's Work*, Athlone Press 1996

Given feminist anger at inequalities and power differences between men and women, it is not surprising that a heated and sometimes vitriolic debate ensued.

Hakim says:

> *The unpalatable truth is that a substantial proportion of women still accept the sexual division of labour which sees home making as women's principal activity and income earning as men's principal activity in life.*
>
> Catherine Hakim, *Key Issues in Women's Work* (1996)

Criticisms of Hakim

There are a range of them mainly from a feminist perspective:

1 Her approach, while detailed in statistics, is not deeply grounded in history. A study of women's history shows that for centuries women's 'choices' have never been as free as men's. This supports the importance of structural constraints on life chances and opportunities which are deeply rooted and cannot be changed by superficial measures such as publicity campaigns and even legislation.
2 She sees women in terms of individuals making choices in a cultural and ideological vacuum. **Irene Breugel** (1996) points to Hakim's view of the supposed economic rationality behind women's choices when these are made as a result of a complex interplay between society and the individual. Feminists have long pointed to the way females from birth are bombarded by a range of social influences including family, education and the media. For example motherhood and childcare images are reinforced by toys such as dolls and ironing boards given to little girls. As shown in other sections of this chapter, the world of work can still be seen in term's of 'women's and men's jobs' despite attempts to change this.

3 Methodologically Hakim uses a quantitative statistical approach to provide empirical evidence for her thesis. Feminist methodologists such as **Liz Stanley** (1990) have pointed to qualitative research methods as a better way of providing an accurate picture of how women live their lives. Standard survey type research is male-constructed and oriented in terms of straightforward answers to questions which does not accord with a female approach. This is where a word like 'choice' becomes contentious as it does not allow for uncovering the stuctural complexities of women's position in society.

4 Crompton (1997) focuses on Hakim's account of women choosing to take up part-time work by using comparative cross-cultural data. She points out that there are wide variations in the number of part-time workers throughout Europe. In Denmark there are far greater numbers of full-time women workers. The differences can be explained in relation to the provision of opportunities, a particular one being childcare for working women which is far superior in Denmark. In this context women's 'choice' is not equal to that of men.

Crompton sees the argument that there are different types of women, some less committed to work than others as simplistic. Women's choices must be seen within structural constraints associated with patriarchy and gender inequalities. She concludes:

> *Preference may shape the employment choices of women, but they do not, contrary to Hakim's assertions, determine them.*

Crompton: *'Gender and Employment' in Social Science Teacher* 26/2, Spairs 1997

Activity

1 Construct a table to summarise the key elements of Hakim's views on women's choices and the opposing arguments.
2 Essay: 'Women's choices today are equal to men, but they choose to concentrate on family and children in preference to work.' Discuss.

PAY

It has been illegal in Britain to pay men more than women since the implementation of the Equal Pay Act in 1975. However despite this, average earnings for women are around 70 per cent of mens'. A simple explanation might be that many more women than men work part time thus accounting for the difference. But even when 'like with like' is compared, that is full-time women workers' earnings compared to full-time men, the proportionate difference is still 79 per cent.

Reasons for the Differences Between Male and Female Earnings

- Far more women in low-paid and low-status jobs (see Horizontal Segregation above, p 74)
- Women majority of part-time workers (80 per cent+)

- In same/similar occupations/professions women in junior positions, men in senior positions (see Vertical Segregation above, p 75)
- Women still the majority of prime childcarers and have to fit work commitments around such responsibilities
- Women still do over 80 per cent of cooking and housework
- Discrimination against women (sexism). Despite Equal Opportunities legislation since 1975 women still experience discrimination, as regular news stories frequently highlight.

  Discriminating on the grounds of gender may be illegal but it is often very difficult to monitor or prove. For example, a man may be chosen for promotion rather than a woman on the grounds of superior qualifications and experience. To challenge this legally may be a messy and protracted business involving hard to obtain quantifiable evidence to support the idea that the woman was as qualified/experienced or better qualified.

- Many women *are* now entering senior managerial positions but the very top ranks are still almost exclusively male. This has been referred to as the 'glass ceiling' where the female reaches so far and can see through it a more senior male above.
- 'Feminised' and 'masculinised' jobs – such issues have been aired previously where particular jobs seen as female such as nursing and secretarial work receive lower pay and status. Historically there are examples to support this as when women become the predominant workers in a previously male domain such as has occurred with clerical work during the twentieth century (see p 00). In teaching the majority of primary school teachers are women compared to the more highly paid university teaching which is predominantly male.

  Another factor is that the sectors of work that are mainly female tend to be those that have a 'caring' or welfare dimension to them. This has been explained as an extension of the housewife and mother role where jobs such as the care of young children, catering and cleaning are seen as fitting in with societal expectations of a woman's role, correspondingly attracting low pay and status. An 'ideal secretary' has been described as an 'office wife' caring for the powerful male manager or director in terms of booking appointments, arranging meetings, sending flowers for his wife's birthday, and even remembering to book a restaurant for his wedding anniversary dinner.

- 'Feminised' and 'masculinised' skills – this connects with the previous point in that it seems no accident that job 'skills', which as Beechey (1982) pointed out are very difficult to pin down, seem to be more highly rated in male occupations thus receiving higher pay and status. A recent argument in the health profession has followed this line with nursing representatives raising issues of whose 'skills' are more important in the long-term care of hospital patients, the nurse (usually female) in constant attendance or the infrequently visiting doctor or consultant (usually male)?

Study point

How would the functionalist theory of stratification (see p 00) respond to this?

SEXISM

It has been noted that discrimination on the basis of gender is against the law but that it is extremely difficult to monitor a large amount of the unofficial or informal discriminatory activity that goes on. The frequent newspaper articles may be the 'tip of the iceberg' with many women experiencing sexism and grudgingly putting up with it as part of the work situation where men are powerful and women comparatively powerless.The increased inroads into more powerful positions made by women may change this in the future. Liberal feminists tend to support this optimistic view whereas radical feminists are more pessimistic, seeing sexism as entrenched in predominantly patriarchal workplaces.

On the most straightforward objective indicator of all, pay, it seems that discriminatory practices are perhaps a significant part of the explanation. Sometimes this occurs in the workplace but can also be in general attitudes to women and their role in the wider society.

Women can be undermined and stereotyped on the basis of physical appearance with terms such as 'bimbo' being applied as a judgement of intelligence. Women in authority can be described as 'bossy' and those in 'tougher' occupations such as the police and armed services as 'over-emotional' in ways rarely experienced by men. Such are the ways that women at work can be put down and given the message to keep out of a 'man's world'.

LEGISLATION

From the 1970s equal opportunities legislation has consistently attempted to eradicate gender inequalities in the workplace. There is no doubt that some success has been achieved; there is greater recognition by many major employers that women must be treated fairly at work. Media and other publicity campaigns such as WISE (Women into Science and Engineering) have raised the profile and public consciousness of women's equality. So there are grounds for optimism but there may still be a fair way to go in eliminating the more subtle forms of 'hidden sexism' that many women still have to undergo.

Global inequalities for women

Anthony Giddens (1994) adds a global dimension to the position of women when he points out that women own 1 per cent of the world's wealth, earn around 10 per cent of the world's income, perform two-thirds of the world's labour, and 'there are no societies in which men do not in some aspects of social life have more wealth, status and influence than women.' (see Globalisation Chapter 10, p 139)

DISCRIMINATION AGAINST ETHNIC MINORITIES AT WORK

In several ways this raises similar issues to the experience of women where ethnic groups are subject to discriminatory practices. In Britain the most common physical characteristic used to stereotype in prejudicial ways is skin colour. Black people from Carribean and African countries have experienced such racism for centuries, such views having roots in our colonial and imperial past. More recently skin colour has combined with cultural and religious differences in white people's attitudes to Asians or more specifically people whose ancestry is from South Asian sub-continent countries such as Bangladesh, India and Pakistan.

Issues of defining ethnic minorities are complex, there are different:

- Religious groups – ranging from Muslims who are the largest in Britain, can be from India, Pakistan or Bangladesh

  Hindus, predominantly from India

  Sikhs , mainly from India
- Urban or rural origins – those groups from rural or village areas tend to stick more closely to traditional ways and are more likely to be in manual occupations or sometimes small 'corner shop' businesses. Those from towns and cities tend to be in the more non-manual professional occupations. However, social class needs to be taken into account as outlined below.
- Countries of origin – a common form of racist abuse is 'Paki' – in fact there are more people from an Indian background than from Pakistan. As well as

Bangladesh, there are Asian heritage people from several African countries including Kenya, Malawi and Uganda.

Interestingly, this latter group do very well both in terms of educational qualifications and professional employment, outperforming the equivalent white population. Pakistani Muslims and Bangladeshis do not fare well in education and the job market compared with Indian origin people. This raises issues of whether social class is the key variable as the latter group tend to be predominantly unskilled working class in ancestry, whereas the former, notably African Asians, are invariably from business and professional class backgrounds.

So it is important to note that what at first appears to be a cultural or ethnic factor is on examination the well-known variable of social class. Even so prejudice on the basis of skin colour cannot be ruled out as a barrier to such groups with much evidence of discrimination among professional groups as well as other sections of the working population.

Racism is the term used for such prejudice although 'race' as such is a discredited term having little scientific validity as an indicator of meaningful differences between people. As has been the case for women, there has been a range of equal opportunities legislation since the 1960s aimed at eliminating racial prejudice which has had some partial effect but with similar problems of monitoring behaviour which is often hidden and discreet:

> The Commission for Racial Equality (CRE) has regularly carried out a series of spot checks on employers to monitor discriminatory practices. One example was when two fictitious applications were sent in response to a job advert for an electronics engineer. One came from a Mr Singh (a Sikh name); the other from a Mr Robinson. Mr Robinson received an invitation for an interview; Mr Singh was rejected. What the CRE had done was to give both similar qualifications and work experience, thus isolating a discriminatory practice. Further still, the letter to Mr Singh was complimentary putting his rejection down to 'competition' and wishing him every success for the future. So a 'real' Mr Singh would have had no idea that he was being discriminated against. Such subtleties indicate the difficulties involved in tackling unequal opportunities.

Another more unusual case reported in 1999 again demonstrates that discrimination continues:

Since 1996 Tahir Hussain has turned racial discrimination into a lucrative activity. He sends in his CV to apply for jobs as a sales administrator plus another with similar qualifications and experience separately under a fictitious pseudonym, usually of a white female. In his latest case he claimed that all 16 people on the shortlist were female. When he is rejected and the fictitious person is invited for interview he has proof of discrimination. So far he has brought 28 cases to tribunals and been awarded almost £50,000 in compensation.

Study point

What does the above case study demonstrate? Racial discrimination against an ethnic person or perhaps positive discrimination in favour of female candidates?

Explain using extracts from the previous section on gender discrimination.

EXPLANATIONS OF ETHNIC INEQUALITIES

Various theories can be applied to explain the position of certain ethnic groups in the labour market. Some are influenced by Marxism such as **Stephen Castles** and **Godula Kosack** (1973) who studied the migratory labour patterns of immigrant ethnic minority workers. They saw discrimination and prejudice against such groups as being rooted in the class structure of capitalism. Such groups form a 'reserve army of labour' (see p 19) used in times of profitability and labour shortages and discarded to unemployment in more difficult economic times. Other ways such a Marxist class analysis is applied is that ethnicity can be used as a divisive factor to undermine the potential unity of the proletariat or working class. Here the idea of 'hegemony', or rule by dominant ideas of the ruling class, can be applied to the way agencies such as the mass media and education can foster and instigate racist stereotypes which result in the working class blaming their exploitation by poor wages and conditions of work, or unemployment on 'them' rather than the capitalist system.

Marxists such as Castles and Kosack use a class analysis to argue that the position of immigrant workers in Britain is no different to that of migrant workers in other countries such as Germany where 'guestworkers' from countries such as the former Yugoslavia and Morocco experience prejudice and discrimination in similar ways. They are all at the bottom of the class structure of a capitalist society, thus forming the most exploitable and exploited groups. Non-Marxists accuse such an approach of 'colour-blindness' and argue that there are qualitative differences in the situation of black and Asian groups in Britain compared to other immigrant workers. Neo-Weberians such as **John Rex** and **Sally Tomlinson** (1979) see subjective elements in how black workers are seen. In Britain this relates to a history and culture of colonialism and imperialism with involvement in such major oppression and subjugation of black people as slavery. This has deeply instilled attitudes of superiority in the white population, which is the roots of racism which continues to the present. Another way of putting it is that white immigrant workers experience less discrimination than black or Asian immigrant workers.

Study point

Consider the two approaches above. Do white migrant workers such as the Irish, Poles and Italians have different experiences in host countries to the equivalent black or Asian groups? Explain in your own words.

Table 6: *Economic activity rates[1]: by ethnic group, gender and age, 1997–98[2]*

GREAT BRITAIN								PERCENTAGES
	MALES				FEMALES			
			ALL AGED				ALL AGED	
	16-24	25-44	45-64	16-64	16-24	25-44	45-59	16-59
White	79	93	78	85	71	76	70	73
Black Caribbean	68	92	72	82	65	78	72	75
Black African	57	85	76	77	..	62	..	56
Other Black groups	68	85	..	78	..	71	..	71
Indian	54	94	73	81	53	70	48	61
Pakistani	54	88	60	72	41	28	..	32
Bangladeshi	58	90	..	70	..	..	..	21
Chinese	40	87	75	71	..	63	..	60
None of the above[3]	54	84	83	76	49	58	63	56
All ethnic groups[4]	77	93	78	85	69	75	69	72

1 The percentage of the population that is in the labour force.
2 Combined quarters: Spring 1997 to Winter 1997–98.
3 Includes those of mixed origin.
4 Includes those who did not state their ethnic group.

SOURCE: *Labour Force Survey, Office for National Statistics, Social Trends 29,* © *Crown copyright 1999.*

AGE INEQUALITY IN THE WORKPLACE

'Silly Old Get' 'Old Codger' are familiar terms of abuse directed at older people. As with women and ethnic minorities, older workers can experience stereotyping and prejudice being judged as too slow and of less ability than a younger worker. Paradoxically, despite increased life expectancy, the age at which one is regarded as 'old' in the employment market has come down. In some newer industries such as computing and finance you can be judged to be 'over the hill' at 40. This has led to debates about a 'Third Age' which occurs after one's career where the opportunity for new pursuits and activity, which might include part-time work, can open up for those made redundant or taking early retirement at around 50.

It has been recognised by psychologists and gerontologists that today's 50 year olds are physically and mentally fitter than any previous generation of that age so the numbers leaving full-time work and careers may seem wasteful. Some employers such as B and Q, the 'Do-It-Yourself' chain, have recognised this in their active campaign to recruit more older workers who are seen as more reliable and conscientious than younger workers.

Study point

Do you agree that older workers are 'more reliable and conscientious' than younger workers? Outline reasons for and against such a view.

Critics might point to the fall in birth rates meaning less younger workers available in the twenty-first century is a factor behind the increased interest in older workers. Also, such workers may be willing to accept lower pay rates if they are receiving pensions or redundancy payments along with lower financial commitments as offspring have grown and left and mortgages may have been paid.

One explanation of age inequalities at work and in society generally stems from the work of the anthropologist **Margaret Mead** who saw a change in societies' attitudes to older people varying from traditional societies through to industrial societies and post-industrial societies:

- Traditional societies: this is where age is venerated and accorded high status. Older people are regarded as possessing wisdom and experience which they pass on to the young. Work skills such as cooking, fishing and hunting are passed on in this way. There is no need for formal education such as schooling.
- Industrial societies: have some elements of traditional society in that, older people still pass on work 'skills' to young, but increased mechanisation and advances in technology mean necessity for formalised school and college

education where specialist skills are taught. As industrialisation encroaches further, the skills of older workers quickly become outdated so they experience redundancy and unemployment in greater numbers.

- Post-industrial societies: increased computerisation and automation replaces more workers. Skills no longer lifelong, have to be constantly updated through retraining and continued education regardless of age. At first older workers suffer disproportionately but the impact gradually spreads to all age groups. Skills in the hands of an elite few 'experts' who command vast salaries. Age becomes younger, with 'burn out' at 30 or 40. Average life expectancy increases, the old become referred to as a 'burden' on the health and welfare system. Falling birth rates may mean older workers re-employed to do menial and unskilled jobs formerly done by the young(see above).

So, in summary, there are similar elements of prejudice and discrimination against older groups of workers as there are against women and ethnic minorities.' Ageism' can now be added to 'sexism' and 'racism' as issues of inequality needing to be addressed so that the term 'over the hill' is no longer part of older workers' experience.

DISABILITY AND OPPORTUNITY

In the employment field, being able-bodied has traditionally been an advantage over the disabled who often experience prejudicial and discriminatory attitudes. The disabled are clearly not a homogeneous group of people. As is the case with ethnic minorities, the term covers a wide range of circumstances and situations. There is even a 'sympathy heirarchy' of disability, for example the blind are high up the list,whereas deafness can be associated with lack of intelligence.The Charity Commission annual publication of accounts reflects this with the Royal National Institute for the Blind collecting far more than the Royal National Institute for the Deaf. Most people are aware of guide dogs for the blind, but few are aware that there are guide dogs for the deaf who warn owners of visitors, door bells and telephone calls.

Occupying a wheelchair quickly shows the disadvantage of mobility as entrances to buildings and places of work are often inaccessible. Recent legislation and social policy has aimed to ensure equality of access but many buildings with internal stairs and entrance staircases testify as to the difficulties wheelchair users face.

Tom Shakespeare (1994) explains how the dominant able-bodied culture objectifies the disabled and gives them a stigmatised identity. From a labelling theory perspective, he argues that disability is socially constructed, and it is society which disables people. Most disabled people are perfectly capable of participating in society, but they are often excluded even down to the physical level of gaining comfortable access to buildings.

It is clear that we are a long way from a society where disability is no hindrance to employment opportunity. The disabled are disproportionately featured in unemployment and unskilled part-time work. It has been argued that technological advances can widen opportunities. The increase in homeworking facilitated by the personal computer and related features such as the Internet could be seen in this way as those with mobility problems can take advantage of circumstances where travel to work and access to buildings has previously created problems. Critics may see such developments as further 'ghettoising' already discriminated against groups. Nevertheless case studies such as the severely disabled world famous astrophysicist Stephen Hawking, author of the best-selling *A Brief History of Time* demonstrates that computers have proved invaluable in enabling the once severely disadvantaged to lead as normal a working life as possible.

Table 7: *Economic activity status of disabled[1] people: by gender, Spring 1998*

UNITED KINGDOM			PERCENTAGES
	MALES	FEMALES	ALL
In employment			
Working in full time	33	16	25
Working part time	5	18	11
All in employment	38	34	37
Unemployed[2]	7	4	6
Economically inactive	54	61	58
All disabled (=100%)			
(millions)	2.8	2.4	5.3

1 Work-limiting disabled. Males aged 16 to 64, females aged 16 to 59. See Appendix, Part 4: Disabled workers.
2 Based on the ILO definition. See Appendix, Part 4: ILO unemployment.
SOURCE: *Labour Force Survey, Office for National Statistics, Social Trends 29, © Crown copyright 1999.*

In 1999 the Disabled Persons Act was implemented, making it the responsibility of employers to show how they were making employment opportunities equal for the disabled and requiring them to set targets for the employment of proportionate numbers.

SEXUALITY AND INEQUALITY AT WORK

Traditionally sexuality has been seen as one's 'private' affair so should have no relevance in the workplace. However, certain occupations such as the armed forces can legally discharge homosexuals as 'prejudicial to the good order of a fighting unit'. This is often accompanied by bizarre assumptions/explanations by high ranking officers which feature the supposed promiscuity of male gays and even expressing worries about communal shower facilities being a source of discomfort to heterosexual soldiers.

The police are another uniformed service and now often assert that sexuality is not an issue in employment and promotion opportunities. Press reports in the summer of 1999 of two lesbian police officers having a church blessing for their marriage may be seen as evidence of this. But formal acceptance in the senior ranks is often not borne out by reality for a gay or lesbian police officer in their daily work. Some officers have hidden their homosexuality behind a smokescreen barrage of heterosexual banter lying about partners and relationships. The police, as studies have shown, is a highly masculinised 'tough' occupation with expectations of behaviour associated with heterosexuality and aggressive masculinity. Up until recently women police officers have experienced such behaviour, and news reports of harassment cases still indicate that despite attempts to create equal opportunities, informal prejudicial practices continue.

The armed services and police may seem exceptional but there are many grounds for considering that similar homophobic practices prevail in more conventional work settings. In heavy physical masculinised manual work, male homosexuality can be reacted to aggressively, making life difficult and occasionally dangerous. Another reaction is to put down the gay by humour and jokes, which requires a similarly humorous response and exaggerated behaviour as with the 'camp', limp-wristed self-mocking gay. This behaviour has antagonised some gay political groups who see this as further adding to the oppression and stereotyping of gay people. Other stereotypes can be associated with particular jobs such as the male ladies' hairdresser and other creative fashion-type occupations. The female bricklayer or lorry driver can be labelled as lesbian for trespassing into supposedly male 'territory'. Things may be improving with greater tolerance and acceptance of homosexuality in a wide range of occupations. A recent newspaper report featured a teacher undergoing a sex change with their head's approval. In the past, homosexuality was a cause for dismissing a teacher. However, even today in supposedly more liberal and tolerant times it is highly likely that many gay and lesbian teachers and other professional workers keep their sexuality hidden and perhaps dread the pupil who may one day ask: 'Sir, are you gay?'

REGIONAL INEQUALITIES

From the early stages of industrialisation to the mid-twentieth century the availability of local raw materials such as iron ore, and power sources such as coal, meant the growth of large industrial centres and regions which employed thousands of workers and created relative prosperity for that area. The decline in stocks of such materials at first did not strongly impact on such regions as they had a vital asset, a skilled labour force, that meant it was still economical to transport raw materials to these centres. In Britain there are several examples of such regions including the North East, famous for shipbuilding and steel, the North West for textiles, Northern Ireland and the Glasgow area for shipbuilding and heavy manufacturing. Since the 1950s, the massive expansion of world trade and cheaper labour costs abroad caused rapid decline in these regions. Britain, once the world's foremost shipbuilding nation, now has little shipbuilding left, and similar developments have affected textiles and train manufacturing. In more recent times, we have seen the decline of Britain as a dominant car manufacturing nation with countries such as Germany and Japan now dominating to the extent that Japanese and German manufacturers have set up car assembly plants in deprived areas such as South Wales and the North East because of government incentives and grants making labour costs cheaper in Britain than at home.

Regional inequalities exist now such that areas of high unemployment are in the formerly prosperous heavy manufacturing regions cited above, leading to a depopulation of these areas mainly by younger migrating workers, adding to existing problems for the older, less employable workers left behind.

Another feature of regional inequalities in employment opportunities is associated with the rise of the computer industry which has no need for a local source of raw materials and skilled labour force. Here factors such as attractiveness of an area's physical surroundings and access via motorways to cultural resources in cities has led to the growth of 'silicon valley' type areas, such as the M4 corridor in Oxfordshire. Another feature of the computer industry is that communication can be accessed from remote areas, so there has been some move by urban 'escapees', sometimes characterised as postmodern new age 'hippies', to 'cottage industries' in remote corners such as the Scottish Highlands and Islands where scenic surroundings and a healthier, less crowded lifestyle are sought as an alternative to stressful city life.

Such developments might be seen as desirable giving workers freedom to live where they wish, but problems concerning freedom of movement arise from inequitable house prices, with property prices in desirable areas with plenty of employment opportunities being double or treble those of depressed high unemployment areas.

SUMMARY

This chapter has examined the relationship between social divisions and work. First the traditional Marxist approach was examined which focuses on the class dimension of work. Distinctions between manual and non-manual pay and conditions were seen as important. There have been recent criticisms of this suggesting that the class divide is now less important as there are now less traditional manufacturing and factory jobs and a far greater number of white collar occupations. More significant divisions at work have emerged. Feminists have highlighted the discrimination and prejudice against women, while others have pointed to similar issues faced by ethnic minorities, homosexuals and the disabled.

STUDY GUIDE

Group work

Class to draw up a list of job titles, then to devise and conduct a survey on social class perceptions. Investigate issues such as whether a manual/non-manual divide is still perceived. What are assumptions about pay and conditions? Are issues of gender and ethnicity discernable?

Practice questions

1 Evaluate the view that class is now a less important source of social division at work.
2 'Women choose to stay at home and care for children.' Discuss.
3 Does ethnicity affect employment opportunities?

Coursework suggestions

1 As a good Sociology student you may have immediately guessed the answers to the conundra on p 73? If not, it is worth noting what reasoning and barriers were involved in getting at the right answers. Try these on friends and family to see how rigid people's ideas on work roles are. Make up your own similar versions, perhaps reversing genders in different stereotypical jobs such as nursing and secretarial.
2 A survey to examine Hakim's ideas on women's 'choice'. You need to think about how you can effectively draw out women's conscious views of their opportunities for work. A good starting point for a pilot study would be your family. A wider perspective could be developed by also drawing on men's views on 'choice'.

7

CONFLICT AT WORK

Introduction

AS YOUR READING of previous chapters has indicated, work can be a cource of conflict for many people. There are a number of sources, depending on what the conflict is about. It is often assumed that the most common source of conflict concerns disputes about pay, but there are several other sources which will be covered in this chapter. These range from conditions of work, including the length of breaks, to managerial style if it becomes too oppressive. The most familiar reaction on the part of workers is the strike, but as will be indicated, there are many other worker responses and often strikes are a last resort. The 1970s may now be seen as the heyday of the strike as an industrial 'weapon' for workers; since then strike records have plummeted. Whether this is a sign of greater worker satisfaction, changes in the law in favouring employers, or fear of loss of job through unemployment, is still subject to debate. Whatever one's political views on the Conservative government of the 1980s and 90s, it is clear that Thatcherist political policies and legislation greatly curtailed workers' rights. Strike records from the 1980s on support this. There are broadly two opposed explanations of this development. Some, politically of the left and sociologically Marxist, hold the view that we have a cowed, fearful or subservient workforce. This approach can be compared with the view that low strike records reflect a more contented workforce earning higher wages. This enables a better standard of living and consumption of a vast array of goods. Such lifestyles would never have been imagined in earlier times.

RESPONSES TO CONFLICT IN THE WORK SITUATION

Many assume that the strike or withdrawal of labour is the most common response to industrial conflict for workers but there are in fact a range of other strategies that can be adopted:

- a lowering of productivity
- absenteeism, sickness and high labour turnover
- industrial sabotage
- work to rule
- airing grievances publicly through use of mass media, marches and demonstrations

Strikes are often 'weapons of last resort' being used when all other avenues have been exhausted. Even in the days when legislation against strikes was less powerful than now, this was the case, perhaps for the obvious or commonsense reason that most workers are reluctant to lose money by not working so would always seek strategies that involved continuing to work. A range of these will be examined in this section.

STRIKES

A strike is the withdrawal of labour by a group of workers to highlight a grievance. It is the most highly visible form of worker industrial action, often associated with a demand for higher pay. There can be other factors precipitating strikes such as a too authoritarian managerial style, conditions of work, cuts in overtime and bonus payments, and pressure to increase productivity.

Strikes have declined as a feature of industrial relations in Britain in the late twentieth century. Some of the reasons for this have already been examined. The strongest link is the political one which sees legislation primarily enacted in the period of Conservative government of 1979–97 whose policies have been described as right-wing and populist. Throughout the 1960s and 70s the popular media waged a campaign against strikes stereotyping industrial workers as greedy and powerful, holding employers and ultimately the country to 'ransom' with their impossible demands. They were often presented as 'sheeplike', led by wild-eyed communist shop stewards and agitators who were using the workers for their own political ends. Politicians of the time were not averse to such stereotyping. During the 1966 National Union of Seamen's strike the then Labour prime minister Harold Wilson described union leaders as plotters in smoke-filled rooms 'holding the country to ransom'. One explanation of the Conservatives' dramatic ousting of a Labour government in 1979 was the so-called 'winter of discontent' when a number of strikes by local authority workers had led to rubbish being left piled in the streets and the recently dead lying unburied in mortuaries. Unsurprisingly the popular press of the day portrayed such issues with their customary graphic and sensationalised details, which no doubt helped the Conservative's electoral gain and led to the social policies we now know as 'Thatcherism'. Such media support and a large majority enabled the government to enact legislation which made the strike an extremely difficult industrial strategy to adopt.

PICKETS, PICKET LINES AND SCABS

Pickets and **Picket lines** are where a group of striking workers stand at the entrance to a firm to try to persuade non-striking workers including office staff and managers not to enter, thus helping to make the strike more effective.

A **scab** is a term of abuse often shouted aggressively and directed at fellow workers who carry on working during a strike.

It is perhaps not surprising that feelings run high when striking workers do not receive any income and suffer hardship. The miners' strike of 1984 saw whole communities in mining areas such as South Wales and Yorkshire rallying round and providing financial and other support for workers in ways that are rare in modern times. This support enabled the strike to continue for several weeks despite strong government measures and a heavy policing presence backed by a predominantly anti-miner press and media.

Use of Mass Media and Public Relations

Because of much of the anti-union propaganda of this earlier era, trades unions have more recently recognised the value of using the mass media as a platform to air grievances and explain their case to the wider public. Public relations and press officers now work on behalf of some unions to serve such a function, perhaps successfully giving balance to the previous pro-employer one-sided accounts.

Key features of 1980s anti-strike policies are:

- the size of picket lines to a maximum of six people. It was argued that this would take out the intimidatory and sometimes threatening dimension of a mass group of pickets trying to prevent non-striking workers from going to work. It was also felt that this would make policing of disputes easier and more effective.
- striking workers are not allowed to picket on the firm's property so entrances and doorways had to be kept clear with pickets remaining at a reasonable distance. Again this was felt to help reduce the intimidatory aspects of picket lines.

- the banning of secondary picketing. This is where a group of workers from another factory or industry turn up to support the picket line of workers involved in an industrial dispute.

- postal ballots of workers so they can have a secret vote on whether to strike. This was seen as an effective political counter to the mass meeting with a 'show of hands' vote after speeches from what right-wingers regarded as left-wing socialist agitators who could unduly psychologically influence people in favour of strike action.

- employers to be given notice well in advance of any strike action. In practice this means that employers can stockpile resources and raw materials to help them weather the impact of strike action.

- employers have to be provided by the union with a full list of members who are to take part in the strike. The declared aim of this was so the employer can contact the employee directly and put their side of the case, so providing a more informed basis for a vote on whether to strike. This was criticised as an intimidatory practice which could lead to the victimisation of individual workers by their employers.

Critics saw all the above policies as part of a media-fuelled backlash severely restricting workers' power and influence and putting control more directly into the employers' hands. They saw this situation as one of a cowed workforce who are intimidated to accept whatever the employer demands with little opportunity to fight back. Neo-Marxist sociologists echo such views and see such trends as an inevitable outcome of a capitalist society. Others are less critical and see such trends as a welcome development where individual workers can make up their own minds about industrial action in an informed manner, free from intimidation from larger groups who may have more political objectives in mind. Some add to the political debate by seeing such policies as aiding democracy as public opinion polls in the 1960s and 70s often reflected the majority view that the unions were too powerful and led by left wing agitators.

More liberal commentators point to the gradual increase in wage levels for most workers in recent years as a key factor in the reduction of strikes since the 1980s. Such views accord with a functionalist sociology that sees a sort of equilibrium having returned to industrial relations. They see many workers as having more stimulating and satisfying work and higher wages than at any time in previous history, enabling a high standard of living compared to the bad old days of exploited labour.

A Neo-Marxist sociological study of strikes by **Richard Hyman** (1984) cites the following characteristics of strikes:

- workers stop work, halting production completely. This makes a strike a powerful weapon compared with the other responses covered below where some elements of production continue, albeit in a restricted form.
- strikes are temporary stoppages. Few last longer than a few days although there have been one or two long-running exceptions that have dragged on for months and years in some cases.
- workers on strike act collectively, guided and organised by trade union officials. The local union official who is a worker in the same company is known as a shop steward. Collective action results in a feeling of togetherness and solidarity in the struggle against the employer.
- strikes involve action by employees and are a reflection of their discontent about pay and/or conditions of work.
- striking workers have goals, such as the desire to settle their grievance through pressure on the employer to negotiate.

WORKING TO RULE AND WORKING TO CONTRACT

A 'work to rule' is a form of industrial action, which sounds contradictory. Working to rule involves employees in a dispute sticking to the companies regulations to the letter which can slow work down. Many work tasks involve cutting corners which can speed things up considerably. Company rules may stipulate carrying out tasks in certain ways for legal, health or safety reasons but turn a blind eye to quicker working practices which increase productivity and don't greatly infringe regulations.

In bureaucratic organisations, such as local government and the civil service, rules are formal and clearly set out. In practice, for similar reasons to above, many are ignored to speed up the work, so 'working to rule' in a dispute about pay or conditions can be highly effective. Employees who obey the rules as laid down formally cannot be reprimanded or disciplined and they still receive pay for their work.

Another more professional dimension has developed in recent years which is 'working to contract'. In former times professionals did not have formal contracts of employment, they were entrusted with professional integrity to do their work with the fullest commitment and responsibility. Since the growth of professional occupations from the 1960s, many of the newer professionals have contracts of employment which stipulate their duties. Often professional commitment is such that tasks are carried out beyond what is stipulated. A good example of this is in the teaching profession where such non-contractual duties, such as running after school clubs and sports teams, have been carried out by enthusiastic teachers. In recent years teachers who have become increasingly involved in conflict with employers from new demands in terms of contracts with longer hours have successfully worked to contract resulting in a decline in out of school activities which heads and parents have expressed concern about as detrimental to pupils and the quality of school life.

LOW PRODUCTIVITY

This can be a symptom of conflict in the workplace where monotonous unfulfilling work results in workers doing the bare minimum required, even advising new workers to 'slow down, you won't get paid any more'. Clearly work on assembly lines, previously discussed, provides an example although in many cases mechanisation can mean that the line controls the pace of work rather than the worker. In such situations employers have tried to make work more fulfilling by means of job enrichment schemes, with varying results. For conflict theorists, low productivity in such work situations is a clear sign of alienation, which cannot be eradicated by such 'tinkering'.

ABSENTEEISM, SICKNESS AND HIGH LABOUR TURNOVER

This can be another manifestation of conflict where workers cannot face their job so take unauthorised absence, feign sickness or simply leave. In several industries Monday is a day when fewer staff turn up for work after the weekend; the view being that after a short break it is difficult to face another day in a boring job. Many such workers take the maximum periods of sickness allowed before meriting a warning or reprimand. In such circumstances productivity will fall.

High labour turnover is another response; workers simply leave. In all but the most unskilled occupations this can be costly to employers as the training of a constant stream of new workers becomes expensive.

INDUSTRIAL SABOTAGE

Laurie Taylor and **Stan Cohen** (1971) were the first British sociologists to highlight industrial sabotage as a form of industrial action. This is perhaps the most visible form of response to conflict where workers either damage the products they make or the machinery they work with. The well-known 'spanner in the works' idea applies here where an apparently 'accidental' sabotaging of a machine can bring workers a welcome respite. On assembly lines when a generator breaks down causing the line to come to a halt, after a few seconds of silence there is often a resounding cheer!

With regard to product damage, cars have had tin cans and bottles placed inside engines, and in the food and catering industry food can be adulterated in sometimes disgusting ways – a form of revenge that can be applied to an awkward customer in a restaurant. It is interesting to note that when such events occur and are related, they often receive an approving response, perhaps a sign of alienation for many as well as an aspect of getting back at 'them' for workers who feel most exploited and resentful.

UNION MEMBERSHIP

Traditionally, trades unions have been seen as representative institutions for mainly manual workers who, in the past, were more likely to be in conflict with employers over pay and conditions. A feature of modern times is the dramatic growth in white collar and professional occupations in the non-manual sectors. Areas such as banking, insurance, health care, teaching and social work have expanded enormously, employing thousands more workers. A proportion of such groups are not highly paid in comparison to manual workers. The result has been a growth since the Second World War of representative white collar unions and professional associations, such that they have become as high profile as manual trades unions in the past. This has been a response to a possible change in the relationship between employer and employee which has become less personal and more oppositional as managers strive to keep wage costs down and white collar and professional employees strive to enhance them along with conditions of work. Clearly factors in the declined personal contact have been the massive expansion in numbers and the growth in size and scale of bureaucratic organisations (see p 58). Other explanations centre around the comparable loss of status of white collar work and the influx of more vulnerable workers such as women and ethnic minorities who require effective representation.

Membership of trades unions fell through the 1990s. Many of the most vulnerable exploited workers do not belong to a union. Some employers do not allow unions to operate in their companies. This may be because the more unscrupulous and oppressive employers do not want such a potential threat in their workplace.

More recently Japanese companies have established branches in the UK, such as Nissan in Sunderland, where union membership is not allowed. A first interpretation could well be that it is an attempt to enforce the power of the company over its employees but a knowledge of Japanese working culture indicates that the idea of belonging to a union is unacceptable as all members of the company are seen to belong on as equal a basis as in a family. Managers and directors wear the same company uniform and eat the same food in the same canteens as the rest of the workforce, in what may appear to be a 'classless' system. Such an approach can be seen as highly paternalistic, but may also be seen as having benefits as Japanese companies are committed to looking after their workers in terms of conditions, pay and job security, very much as the ideal parent looks after all its family members. Sceptics from a Marxist perspective may say that is all very well so long as capitalism succeeds and workers can be offered reasonable pay and conditions when profits are high, but such loyalties as described can just as easily melt away in more difficult economic circumstances, resulting in factory closures and worker redundancy.

Global companies are increasingly powerful in economic and political terms having vast wealth and financial power at their disposal. This includes their willingness to move production either to regions with newer global markets or where low wage costs and a compliant labour force exist. Some have explained the dramatic rise in Far Eastern and Pacific Rim economies in such terms. More recently the rise of China as a major producer in the global marketplace has resulted in forecasts of its potential to dominate world markets within a few years. Clearly such developments will have an impact on workplaces throughout the world and may be symbolic of forces that are difficult for workers and their representative unions to resist.

SUMMARY

This chapter has examined the causes and consequences of conflict in the workplace in modern societies. It has been recognised that conflict is a significant feature of all types of work. The struggle for higher pay, better conditions and opportunities for workers has been a familiar feature of work in industrial societies for many years. In manual occupations there are such strains as hard, physically demanding work and boring monotonous work on an assembly line. Other occupations have their sources of conflict in familiar areas such as pay and conditions, as well as the more recent pressure of increased hours and extra demands causing stress and related illnesses. Marxist-influenced approaches see conflict as an inevitable feature of all capitalist socities which can only be eradicated by the establishment of a socialist society; feminists and ethnicity theorists highlight the pressures on women and ethnic minorities. More optimistic views are that the sources of conflict are diminishing as we work together in 'partnership' based on reasonable remuneration leading to higher standards of living.

Postmodernists see rapidly changing arenas for conflict where old divisions are less in evidence. Globalisation leads to competitive struggles between massive corporations which vie with each other in a shrinking world of rapid communications, via computers and the Internet. Some groups in the forefront of such developments will gain and possibly women are the best at adapting to the requirements of flexibility and change. Such developments mean that the old sources of conflict centred around the traditional management/shopfloor divide and differences between manual and non-manual work become increasingly less relevant. The institutions such as trades unions and professional associations which were formed in such arenas will have to adapt and accommodate to such a rapidly changing world.

Group work

1 Possibly using some of the class with part-time jobs, discuss whether conflict is a strong feature of workplaces. How do workers express grievances about areas such as pay and conditions?
2 Examine statistics of strike records and evaluate their accuracy as a measure of conflict.

Practice questions

1 Compare and contrast Marxist and Weberian explanations of conflict in the workplace.
2 'Social class has been replaced by other inequalities at work as the key modern sources of conflict.' Discuss.
3 Examine the view that recent British strike records show a decline in conflict at work.

Coursework suggestions

Design and conduct a survey to examine people's experience of conflict in the workplace. What are the key causes? For example, is it relationships between people? Increased demands and pressures from employers? For women, worries associated with childcare?

8

UNEMPLOYMENT

Introduction

UNEMPLOYMENT TOUCHES ALL our lives. Among your own group of relatives and friends it is highly likely that some have experienced or are currently experiencing unemployment. What are the reasons for this? Is it redundancy because of technology replacing human skills? Early retirement, for some as young as 50 (a form of 'hidden' unemployment)? The lack of skills? For a young person lack of experience? For a woman 'hidden' unemployment caused by lack of adequate childcare provision? Discrimination and racism? Disability?

Many would see unemployment as a major social problem. Sociologically, having a job is a source of one's position, status and esteem in society. Your position in the class structure is determined by your occupation. Economically, work means the ability to earn a living, support dependants and buy consumer goods. More social features of having a job are the sense of belonging to society and the opportunity to interact with fellow workers.

Different approaches to unemployment
- Sociological explanations of unemployment include seeing it as a 'necessary evil' produced by technological advances bringing mechanisation and automation. This can be compensated for by education and reskilling unemployed workers to cope with such demands, so ideally unemployment should be short-lived and temporary.
- Marxist approaches see unemployment as an inevitable feature of a capitalist society which uses a pool of unemployed workers as a 'reserve army of labour' (see p 19), partly as a threat to other workers in terms of their wage and related demands.
- Feminists point to the 'hidden' aspects of unemployment affecting women who may not appear in official government statistics but are trapped at home and unable to work because of inadequate childcare provision.

- Ethnicity theorists point to the higher proportions of some ethnic minorities among the unemployed as evidence of discrimination and racism in the labour market.
- Interactionists/interpretivists point to the labelling process attached to the unemployed creating them as deviants and social outsiders.

Table 6: *Concepts, theories, issues and figures in this chapter*			
KEY CONCEPTS	THEORIES	KEY ISSUES	KEY FIGURES
Deskilling	Neo-Marxist	Workers have been replaced by technology thus raising unemployment levels	Braverman
Harm and costs		Unemployment is physically, psychologically and socially destructive.	Kay Laurance Sinfield
Youth			Roberts
Underclass	Right realism	Unemployment in urban communities has led to rise of underclass, single parenthood, rising crime and drug abuse	Murray

MEASURING UNEMPLOYMENT

An initial problem is the familiar one of accuracy when using official statistics. Unemployment statistics are published monthly by the government but are seen to be flawed and a probable underassessment for the following reasons:

- only those officially registered as unemployed by claiming state benefits are in the figures
- men of over 60 years are not counted
- young people under 18 are also not included
- housewives and mothers could well seek work if childcare provision was more accessible, for example more firms providing workplace crèches. At present they are not registered or counted as unemployed
- some registered as long-term sick and disabled may take up work if opportunities and facilities were better
- many who continue in education as students post-16 would have taken up work if it were available
- many older people are fit and active well past retirement age and would take up or continue employment if it were available.

Because of the above reasons the Trades Union Congress estimate that 'real' unemployment is probably treble that portrayed by official figures. All governments strive to reduce figures, sometimes artificially as above, but claim 'real' success as a sign of policy achievements.

THE CAUSES OF UNEMPLOYMENT

Unemployment rates have varied according to a range of factors. A booming economy and increased production and consumption can lead to falling unemployment. Declining industries and falling consumption of particular products, as with bicycles earlier in the twentieth century, can raise unemployment.

Marxists associate mass unemployment with the capitalist system of production. The inevitable logic of capitalism is that profits are maximised by reduction in worker and wage costs. Technology can be used in this way as Braverman argued (see p 44). Another feature previously aired is that unemployed workers can be used in times of a boom in the economic cycle and as an example to employed workers at other times to curtail their possible wage and related demands.

Functionalist sociologists see unemployment as perhaps unfortunate but partly inevitable. They would stress its temporary features for most workers as they are re-educated and retrained for newer skills and industries. They would also highlight improved redundancy and early retirement packages, state benefits and support, access to cheaper travel, leisure and healthcare (eg exemption from prescription charges) as ameliorating factors for the longer-term unemployed.

Another aspect of the functionalist view is that machines can take over boring and monotonous tasks leaving opportunities for more creative and interesting work by means of retraining those who are made redundant.

WHO ARE THE UNEMPLOYED?

SOCIAL CLASS AND UNEMPLOYMENT

Contrary to media publicity about rising unemployment among executives and managers, in social class terms unemployment affects a far greater proportion of the lower working class, that is unskilled manual workers, in comparison with middle-class white collar workers. Another dimension of this is that the more educationally qualified have lower unemployment rates, which also challenges publicity about graduate unemployment. It would appear that government policies to expand educational opportunities for all is correct, but some observers have pointed out that this has led to an over-qualified workforce with graduates now doing jobs in the white collar sector which previously were filled by less qualified workers. For example, the teaching profession from the 1980s became all-graduate entry, and more recently in nursing the aim is to make it a graduate profession with degrees in Nursing as entry qualifications.

From the 1970s on Britain's manufacturing industry has seen massive closures of factories and mills, such that today a minority of workers are in this sector, leading to some commentators stressing that we are now no longer a manufacturing nation.

The optimistic view is that such redundant workers have been retrained and reskilled for jobs elsewhere, for example in the expanded white collar sector. More pessimistic commentators point to the large growth in official unemployment from the 1980s on, as well as the 'hidden' dimension of early retirement, unrecorded female unemployment and young people.

UNEMPLOYMENT AND POVERTY

Contrary to popular myth unemployment is not featherbedded by generous state benefits. Over 95 per cent of workers will be worse off financially if they become unemployed, the exception being those in low skilled, low paid occupations with dependants. Various governments have tried to deal with this apparent anomaly that discourages a small minority from working by measures such as family credit allowances paid to low wage earners to boost their income beyond state benefit levels.

AGE AND UNEMPLOYMENT

Young people under 18 years are not included in the official unemployment figures, but this does not necessarily mean they are unaffected by unemployment. Most young people of 16–19 years are pursuing further educational qualifications so are not in full time employment. Gradually this age group is increasing to the mid-20's as more continue to university education. This could be interpreted as another disguised form of unemployment defended by a form of functionalist view that there is a need for an educated, skilled graduate workforce to cope with the demands of an advanced, highly technological society.

As more go on to study for degrees, increasingly interrupted by temporary employment to finance their studies, the future could well mean a workforce that does not enter full-time career employment until the mid- to late-20s. Future predictions are that the three-year full-time degree will diminish as people have to take up temporary employment to finance their studies, so flexible degrees and part-time study will become the norm. We could well follow a similar trend to Germany where degrees can take up to 8 years to complete and many young Germans can reach 30 years old before they start a full-time career or professional job.

ETHNICITY AND UNEMPLOYMENT

An earlier section highlighted the discrimination faced by ethnic minorities in the competition for jobs, citing factors such as racism and stereotyping affecting black and some Asian groups. It is not therefore surprising to find that such groups have higher rates of unemployment compared with dominant white groups:

Table 8: *Unemployment rates[1]: by ethnic group and age, 1997–98[2]*					
GREAT BRITAIN					PERCENTAGES
	16-24	25-34	35-44	45-59/64[3]	ALL AGED 16-59/64[3]
White	13	6	5	5	6
Black	39	18	12	16	19
Indian	18	7	6	7	8
Pakistani/Bangladeshi	29	16	13	26	21
Other groups4	22	13	10	8	13
All ethnic groups[4]	14	7	5	5	7

1 Unemployment based on the ILO definition as a percentage of all economically active. See Appendix, Part 4: ILO unemployment.
2 Combined quarters: Spring 1997 to Winter 1997–98.
3 Men up to the age of 64, women up to the age of 59.
4 Includes those of mixed origin.
5 Includes those who did not state their ethnic group.
SOURCE: *Labour Force Survey, Office for National Statistics, Social Trends 29, © Crown copyright 1999.*

REGIONAL UNEMPLOYMENT

Unemployment varies across regions with highest rates in traditional industrial areas such as the North East of England and lowest rates in the new technology and service industry centres, such as the South East. As workers migrate to such areas the result has been declining population in cities such as Liverpool and growth in cities such as London, Oxford and Cambridge. A reflection of this is the escalating property prices and accommodation costs in these areas which create added difficulties for workers from other regions. An additional 'Catch 22' situation sometimes faced is that an employer will not hire someone without an address while correspondingly rented accommodation or a mortgage cannot be obtained without a job. This can result in some workers returning to long-term unemployment in their home region. Despite this demographic trends show a clear population shift from areas of high unemployment to areas of low unemployment. The result is already seen in an overcrowded South East with jammed roads and vastly overpriced housing and accommodation compared with impoverished areas of high unemployment and rapidly deteriorating housing stock.

Governments and local authorities have attempted to correct some of these trends by regeneration policies aimed at attracting industries to areas of high unemployment. They have provided incentives to employers in terms of grants and support funding with varying degrees of success. Another feature was the relocating of government departments to higher unemployment areas.The Department of Social Security, which deals with National Insurance contributions, has its headquarters and central records office in Newcastle. Up to the 1990s such policies were aimed mainly at home industries and businesses but since then such policies have become more global with encouragement to employers such as Japanese car manufacturers to site factories in Sunderland and South Wales.

CONSEQUENCES AND SOCIAL COSTS

The following chilling quote is a commonly recognised feature of the despair of unemployment which Lord Beveridge (1879–1963), the architect of the British Welfare State in the post-Second World War period identified as a social evil to be eradicated:

There are no good aspects about being unemployed. It's like doing time ... there's no way out of it. You've no hope for the future. You're better off dead.

32-year-old man, unemployed for five years quoted from Tess Kay (1989)

It has been consistently stated throughout this book that having a job or occupation is an important source of a sense of belonging and identity in society. It is not therefore surprising that being unemployed has deleterious effects on the people concerned. There are very few people who happily accept their unemployment despite occasional sensational tabloid stories featuring contented 'scroungers', such as eco-warriors, living off state benefits.

Unemployment affects people negatively at a number of levels:

1 Biological and physiological

Such a link may at first seem surprising as we may not expect unemployment to have physical affects. The measure of this comes from ill-health and illness records which clearly show that the unemployed have higher rates of all kinds of illness, even for the extremes of life-threatening conditions such as heart problems and cancer. At a less serious level it is well-known that unemployment can lead to some becoming apathetic about their physical appearance, such as men not shaving regularly, which can affect how prospective employers judge them. Long-term unemployment can result in a 'Why bother?' attitude, leading to neglect of physical appearance and health where even eating and drinking healthily becomes unimportant.

Jeremy Laurance (1986) highlighted the health effects of unemployment noting an increase in GP visits and hospital admissions after a major employer closed down in a small English town. He pointed to a range of studies that support the view that unemployment is a cause of ill-health.

2 Psychological

This can relate to **1** and **4**. The unemployed are more likely to suffer from depressive mental illnesses. In some tragic extreme cases unemployed people commit suicide. Suicide rates are in greater proportion than for the employed. Poor self-image and a feeling of worthlessness result in a downward psychological spiral into despair which those in paid work rarely experience.

Unsurprisingly, attitudes are mainly negative either about the current situation or future job prospects which may become a noticeable hindrance in a job interview. Employment officers and counsellors are trained to help people develop a more positive outlook and gain in confidence in their search for work. However this is not an easy task, particularly in areas of mass unemployment where job prospects are low.

However it has been pointed out by researchers such as **Adrian Sinfield** (1981) that the psychological affects of unemployment can vary between different individuals and groups. For example, in an area where unemployment is high among young people the effects may be less than for a middle-aged manager who is made redundant in a prosperous area. **Ken Roberts** (1984) reinforces this in a study of the young unemployed which shows a level of resilience and acceptance. However, **Lea and Young** (1984) disagree highlighting how unemployment marginalises the young creating a subculture of despair which can lead to the tragic cases of suicide regularly featured in the mass media.

3 Economic

The majority of people are worse off financially if they are unemployed. **Melanie White** (1990) cites a study showing that over two-thirds of families with parents under 35 were in debt after 3 months unemployment. In many cases income can be as little as a quarter or less of previous paid earnings, clearly contributing to the circumstances in **1**, **2** and **4** (below). Very few people are better off despite tabloid attention to so-called dole 'winners'. It used to be that a minority of unskilled low-wage earners or those with many dependants could be better off claiming state benefits, but recent government policies such as working family credit payments and the minimum wage of £3.60 per hour for adult workers, have been aimed at making working more profitable for all.

Being unemployed is a cause of financial stress and hardship which often leads to poverty. Lack of money is a key source of strains in family life and relationships (see **4** below). This can be added to in a high consumption society such as ours where the constant message from media and other sources is to buy and spend on a multitude of goods. Even children are drawn into this with their increased awareness of the correct brand or label in toys and clothes. The age when such awareness develops is constantly reducing with even toddlers and babies becoming targetted as wearers of designer garments and other merchandise.This creates additional pressures on unemployed parents as they walk past the shopping centres bustling with the consuming working population.

Activity

Contact your local Social Security Office or Welfare Agency to find out unemployment benefit rates for single and married people with dependants. Contact your local Chamber of Commerce, Job Centre or investigate through library sources what local average pay rates are for manual and non-manual work and compare the two to investigate the financial loss associated with unemployment. (Don't forget that wage earners with children may be entitled to additional Working Family Credit payments to help with childcare.) Work together to present a class report on the financial affects of unemployment. Write a response in one or two paragraphs using such evidence to reply to someone in a bus queue who says, 'I don't know why I bother working, you're better off on the dole these days.'

4 Sociological

There is considerable overlap between all four levels and in a sense they all combine together at the sociological level. Unemployment means a lack of esteem and a loss of status within society. In past times of high unemployment, such as the 1930s when whole working class communities and neighbourhoods were out of work, there was a sense of togetherness in adversity which helped people to cope. There was less stigma in such communities when the majority were affected.

In modern societies the fragmentation of communities associated with urban renewal programmes and the increased privatisation of personal lives within nuclear family households have led to a loss of neighbourhood contacts. We are now more likely to make friends and social contacts through work and related organisations such as schools and colleges which are increasingly at a distance from where we live. Becoming unemployed means this vital social contact is lost and the neighbourhood cannot replace this. This adds to the sense of isolation of the unemployed who are left with only their immediate family for support.It is perhaps unsurprising in such circumstances (with added dimensions such as financial hardship outlined in **3**) that divorce and family breakdown is higher. The previously mentioned fragmentation of communities and population movement has led to neighbourhoods where there can be a mix of the employed and unemployed, with the latter in an increasingly isolated minority.

CRIME AND THE UNEMPLOYED

Neo-conservative social scientists such as **Charles Murray** (1989) have highlighted the development of an unemployed 'underclass' in deprived urban areas of countries such as Britain and the USA.This underclass is seen as 'criminogenic', ie a producer and reproducer of criminality through the generations. Murray has provided lurid accounts of underclass children, some barely beyond the toddler stage, roaming the streets late at night engaged in anti-social acts, destined to become the criminals of tomorrow.

Poverty and associated financial and psychological stress has been used to explain higher crime rates among the unemployed. There is a certain commonsense logic in the idea that if money cannot be earned legally then a proportion of people may turn to crime to support themselves and their families. As you will discover when you study the sociology of crime you will find a wide range and number of explanatory causes, with unemployment being one among many. Associated with possible involvement in crime is drug abuse which in the case of the unemployed can be a response to the despair and deprivation experienced, as films such as *Trainspotting* graphically illustrate.

SOCIAL POLICY ON UNEMPLOYMENT

Traditionally political parties in Britain could be identified in terms of left- and right-wing policies on unemployment. In simple terms, parties of the left, such as

Labour, looked to increased state control and ownership of business and industry so that labour markets could be controlled to reduce the rates of unemployment. In high unemployment areas, the state could create jobs by public works schemes, such as house and road building, financed out of taxation. The desired aim was the Keynesian idea of 'Full Employment' with the few thousand unemployed being mainly those temporarily between jobs. Critics saw the creation of vast bureaucratic government departments which were inefficient and costly driving up taxes for those in work. Another aspect of left-wing policies was to improve benefit levels by means of additions to basic benefits based on previous earnings so unemployment did not necessarily lead to abject poverty.

Right wing policies saw the key to solving unemployment in terms of tax cuts for the able and talented in business and industry. The higher income from tax cuts was seen as an incentive for such people to be more creative and hardworking, resulting in their increasingly sucessful enterprises expanding and needing more workers, hence reducing unemployment. In addition to this, benefits should be kept lower than wage rates to act as incentives for people to work and there was an attack on 'inefficiency' in government departments which would help reduce costs. Another 'right wing' dimension was an attack on dole 'cheats' who worked and claimed benefits, so extra surveillance and detection posts were created to deal with this identified 'problem'. Defenders of such policies point to the reduction of unemployment through the period of Conservative government in the 1980s and early 90s. Critics say that the unemployment figures were deliberately 'massaged' excluding categories of people such as males over 60 years and the under 18s (see p 102). The 'real' figure for unemployment was much higher.

RECENT POLICIES

A range of policies to deal with unemployment have been implemented since the election of a New Labour government in May 1997. Ideologically commentators have described these policies as a shift to the right in political terms where ideas such as the American 'Welfare to Work' and 'New Deal' policies have caused critics to talk in terms of the unemployed being forced into low-paid, insecure and often temporary jobs through 'Restart' interviews and related pressures. Ministers and government spokespersons have defended such policies as dealing with the 'real world' of competition in globalised labour markets. The Chancellor of the Exchequer has talked in terms of policies which aim to get people off unemployment benefit and into retraining and newly created jobs. Such debates often involve postmodern images invoking a new situation where a 'Third Way' is required to deal with unemployment in a rapidly changing world of high tech communications and innovations, and globalised labour markets where stable employment and career 'jobs for life' are a thing of the past. Critics say that what has occurred is a reduction in official unemployment levels but the majority of the 'new' jobs are low skilled, short-term, low-paid and part-time.

SUMMARY

This chapter has addressed a topic which many see as a key social problem of modern times. Most sociologists see work as an essential element of human societies providing social position, esteem and status. It is clear that being unemployed usually means a dramatically reduced standard of living, resulting in stress on unemployed individuals and their families. Unsurprisingly health and psychological problems often develop and an unfortunate few are driven to suicide.

From the mid-twentieth century, many experts highlighted technological advances, particularly in the computing field, which would force increased numbers into structural unemployment. Throughout the industrialised world unemployment rates rose steadily through the twentieth century, but in the later years a succession of right-wing policies, such as tax cuts for the rich, were seen as having an impact, some hailing a distinct reversal of rising unemployment trends. Currently unemployment in Britain is around 1.2 million which compares to almost 3 million in the early 1980s. However, critics point to the number of changes in the way statistics are compiled with significant groups, such as males over 60 being removed from the figures. Feminists have pointed to the number of women with children who are not registered as unemployed but would take up work if affordable and convenient childcare was available. Others point to the dramatic growth in low-paid, part-time and temporary jobs which more people are forced into as a result of more recent government policies such as the 'Welfare to Work' and the 'New Deal' policies of the British New Labour government. Expanded length of education to the late 20s and early retirement and redundancy from 50 onward means a condensation of the age labour cohort into the years 25–50. Some predict this may reduce even further.

So it would seem that the future for increased numbers of those in the labour market will be one of either unemployment, with all the pressures that involves, or low-paid low-skill work which is insecure and often short-lived, a very different situation to earlier times when school leavers looked to a future of stable jobs and careers in one occupation, with steadily rising incomes and standards of living.

STUDY GUIDE

Group work

A role-playing exercise where a range of workers experiencing unemployment are covered, such as a bricklayer, a factory worker, a schoolteacher, a manager and a shopworker. Each group to examine details from this chapter to include in their group character. Include old and young workers, men and women.

Practice questions

1 'Unemployment is one of the great social evils of our time.' Examine sociological responses to this view.
2 Assess the New Labour government's policy on reducing unemployment aiming for full employment and getting people back to work.
3 'The old stable jobs have disappeared for ever, and been replaced by short-term, low-paid and low-skilled work.' Discuss.

Coursework suggestions

You need to be aware of the sensitivities of conducting research on unemployment. It would be unethical to select unemployed people to investigate their feelings or attitudes. Examine political approaches to the problem of unemployment to investigate whether a target of full employment, ie around 1 million is socially acceptable.

9

LEISURE

Introduction

WHAT ARE YOUR leisure activities? This is a common question which can occur in job interviews or on first meeting someone. Answers can vary from specific sports or hobbies such as playing cricket or cycling to more open-ended activities such as listening to music, reading, 'clubbing' and 'socialising'.

This chapter perhaps presents a more optimistic picture of society than the previous one as its focus is on something that most enjoy and make choices about. Leisure may seem to be a straightforward matter of choice about what we do in our free time. However this supposed choice is not equally available to all, as sociologists have pointed out. There is also the image in modern times of an 'explosion of leisure', reflecting a massive increase of choice and opportunity now sometimes referred to as a 'leisure industry'. In terms of scale and financial investment this latter description seems very apposite.

Sociologists have studied leisure in a variety of ways focusing on the following areas:

- The relationship between work, non-work time such as travel to work, and leisure
- The so-called 'democratisation of leisure' where the expansion of leisure opportunities associated with industrialisation has made leisure available to all
- Leisure and the life cycle covering such issues as childrearing and ageing
- Leisure as compensation for unfulfilling work, a chance to escape
- The relationship between leisure activities and social divisions and inequalities along lines of social class, gender, ethnicity, age, sexuality and disability
- Leisure as an industry making profits for 'new' capitalists who engage in building leisure empires alongside a variety of other diverse business ventures

- More recently, postmodern approaches have linked leisure to social identity which now relates to modern patterns of mass consumption and lifestyle.

Table 9: *Concepts, theories, issues and figures in this chapter*			
KEY CONCEPTS	THEORIES	KEY ISSUES	KEY FIGURES
Work, non-work and leisure		Time in industrial societies seen as separate blocks	Parker
Work–leisure relationship		Type of work affects our leisure	
Democratisation of leisure	Functionalist	Massive expansion of cheap leisure has made it available to all	Roberts
Family life cycle		Leisure patterns change through family life cycle	Rapoports
Alienation	Neo-Marxist	Alienation produced under capitalist work conditions spills over into the whole of life	Wilensky
Class-based leisure		Inequalities of leisure based on class conflict	Clarke and Critcher
Gender	Feminist	Women's leisure different to men's. Often associated with home and children, or body image.	Deem
Patriarchy		Men control and influence women's opportunities for leisure.	Green
Ethnicity		There are differences in opportunity for leisure. Ethnic minorities are stereotyped.	Fleming Cashmore
Youth	Postmodern	Cross-cultural fusion of style and taste in youth culture	Gilroy Hebdige

DEFINING LEISURE

The word leisure is often associated with choice and free time, as something which occurs outside working hours. It is seen as sometimes having a compensatory function, as exemplified by the desk-bound office worker who runs marathons at weekends or the builder's labourer playing darts in his local. Leisure often implies activity so we talk in terms of leisure pursuits which distinguishes it from time outside work which also involves activities such as eating and sleeping. We recognise leisure as compartmentalised in time so parts of evenings and weekends are ascribed as leisure time. Ideas of freedom and choice are central to how we perceive leisure, so washing up and ironing clearly do not count (see 'non-work time' below). In present times the word leisure covers a wide array of activities ranging from the specific and regular, such as sports and hobbies, to less specific and irregular such as tourism and holidays. Some see going out with friends, watching television and listening to music as leisure activities. Such pursuits are less active and may not be seen as leisure by others.

As with the definition of work another aspect of defining leisure is that it can be relative, differing between individuals. For example, one person may describe gardening as an enjoyable leisure activity or hobby,whereas another may dislike it and describe it as 'hard work'. Someone riding a bicycle may see it as a cheap environmentally friendly form of transport, someone else may ride a bicycle to get fit or as a sport.

TIME

Stanley Parker (1971) categorised our daily lives in terms of work, non-work and leisure time. Non-work time includes getting ready for and travelling to work, eating, sleeping and household tasks. In a later work (1983) he further developed non-work time into work-related obligations, non-work obligations such as cleaning windows or walking the dog, and existence where eating and sleeping are examples.

EARLY SOCIOLOGICAL APPROACHES TO LEISURE

THE RELATIONSHIP BETWEEN WORK AND LEISURE

It often used to be assumed that there was no connection between the job you do and the leisure you could take part in, a key element in the idea of choice and free time. Since then notions of leisure choice being related to physical aspects of work and as compensatory have developed.

Parker (1971) was one of the first British sociologists to examine the relationship between certain types of work and leisure patterns. In a small study which had methodological weaknesses he compared residential childcare officers, bank clerks and those in 'extreme' occupations such as mining and deep sea fishing. He found a clear connection between such occupations and approaches to leisure which challenged ideas that leisure choice was in some way random and unpredictable. He devised a model which aimed to encapsulate three broad types of work–leisure relationship:

1 Extension

This applied to those occupations such as residential childcare where the boundaries between work and leisure are unclear. Such workers in their 'free time' may be organising a trip or a sports activity, or reading a work-related journal, or studying for a further professional qualification. There is a positive attitude to their work and a reasonable sense of satisfaction.

2 Opposition

This relationship involves more negative attitudes and dislike of work which is physically demanding and sometimes dangerous. Here leisure is seen as an escape from such pressures such that certain workers, such as deep sea fishermen, have what has been termed by **Jeremy Tunstall** (1962) as an 'explosion of leisure' possibly involving heavy drinking in pubs and clubs, spending large amounts of money. North Sea oilworkers in the heyday of high pay were reported as burning £20 banknotes on the train home and driving cars into lakes when they returned from leave, signs of wasteful, extravagant consumption which reflected the pressures of their work.

3 Neutrality

Here attitudes to work are neither strongly positive or negative,for example bank clerks are ambivalent about their work. Parker saw this type of work as not strongly affecting leisure as in **1** and **2** above. The routine of such work could result in fairly passive leisure pursuits such as watching television or going to the pub.

Evaluation

While Parker's work was important for pointing to a link between occupation and leisure which had a degree of plausibility, he was criticised for over-generalisation and selective choice of a few possibly untypical jobs. There were also methodological weaknesses concerning small sample size and scant consideration to other sociological variables such as age, social class, family life cycle and gender. Attitudes to work on a positive or negative scale are difficult to pin down precisely, for example some bank clerks may enjoy their work and be looking to managerial responsibility in the future, whereas some childcare officers may dislike their work with unruly youngsters, finding it stressful and demanding, and seek escape in their leisure time in similar ways to those in extreme occupations.

Another factor to consider is the dramatic rise in range and diversity of leisure opportunities since Parker's study was carried out.

THE INCREASED AVAILABILITY AND CHOICE OF LEISURE IN MODERN SOCIETIES

Roberts (1986) picks up on the objection to the narrowness of Parker's model in categorising work–leisure relationships. He points to the vast array of leisure activities available in the late-twentieth century which gives all members of society a wide range of choice in their leisure pursuits. Many leisure activities are relatively cheap and accessible, such as dining out, going for country walks and even foreign holidays, making a 'democracy of leisure', reflecting a pluralistic society. Such newer forms of consumption-style leisure patterns have replaced traditional class-divided activities such as pigeon racing for the working class and fell-walking for the middle classes (see 'Social Class' below). A good example of the 'new' leisure activities is football supporting, which was once clearly a working class pursuit. Now football is a more 'classless' mass participation spectator sport which has enabled it to become a massive leisure industry.

LEISURE AND THE FAMILY LIFE CYCLE

Robert and **Rhona Rapoport** (1975) pointed to the relationship between leisure and the family life cycle. This emphasised factors such as age, child rearing obligations and gender as affecting choice and types of leisure pursuits. A young childless couple may be able to have similar leisure pursuits to when they were single, so working at the gym or going to the pub to meet friends continues. A dramatic change can occur with the birth of children, more particularly for mothers whose time becomes dominated by their offspring. In modern families more young fathers are drawn into family activities in the evenings, at weekends and during holidays. Sporting activities and playing music tends to decline.

For mothers and fathers leisure activities such as swimming, walking and cycling become activities involving children, not forgetting the feminist perspective that women's time is more dominated by catering for children's leisure. At later stages in the life cycle, children leave home and middle-aged couples take part in leisure and holidays without them. In old age stereotypical activities such as bowling and ballroom dancing may be taken up; some of these activities being very different from those of their youth.

The Rapoports focus strongly on family life in a stereotypical nuclear family as a norm for the majority. It could now be argued that rising rates of relationship breakdown, and the growth in childless women and people choosing to remain single mean such generalisation is inappropriate. It could be suggested that the expansion of leisure opportunities combined with female control over fertility and their financial independence through work has been a factor in the growth to one quarter of women remaining childless and both males and females opting to remain single either to their mid-30s on or in some cases for life. In other words getting married young and raising children has become less attractive in a world where consumption lifestyles and participatory leisure opportunities, such as sports and foreign travel are available to all.

Activity

Discuss the arguments for and against this latter view with friends and parents. For example, is it all right for 50 year olds to go clubbing? In the late 1990s the Rolling Stones, aged 50 years plus, were satirised and described as 'Rock Dinosaurs' in reviews of their UK tour for not 'growing up' and for playing rock music when some were grandparents. Are such views 'ageist'? What is wrong with older people participating in rock music?

SOCIAL DIVISIONS AND INEQUALITY AS FACTORS AFFECTING LEISURE

SOCIAL CLASS

Up to the late-twentieth century many leisure pursuits could be clearly associated with social class. Working class leisure included activities such as pigeon racing, allotment gardening to grow vegetables, darts and playing bingo, whereas golf, tennis, squash and bridge were predominantly middle class pursuits. Even a visit to the local pub could involve separate rooms along class lines, with the more middle class drinking in the carpeted lounge bar while the working class drinkers were in the vaults room, sometimes nicknamed the 'rough end'. One obvious factor in class-divided leisure was the cost involved. Playing golf or squash involves membership fees and purchasing equipment such as a set of golf clubs along with appropriate clothing and footwear. This can be compared with the cheapness of playing darts or bingo.

However beyond this there are additional behavioural and social dimensions to leisure activities which can still persist today. Membership of a golf or tennis club does not only involve paying membership fees but requires an application to join endorsed by two existing members. In the more exclusive golf clubs members are predominantly from the business and professional classes so a working class applicant would not have members in his circle of friends. An additional factor is the cultural and behavioural expectations of such clubs where club dinners, formal dress codes in the clubhouse and language and titles such as 'lady captains' give an aura of middle class respectability.

Although some of the above vestiges of class-related leisure still remain, some sociologists and commentators see the emergence of a less class-based world of leisure from the 1970s on. Following on from Roberts' ideas outlined above on the massive expansion of choice and the 'democratisation' of leisure such commentators view this expansion in opportunity as leisure becoming relatively classless. The encroachment of the middle classes into football, which up to the 1960s was almost exclusively working class is one example which has already been referred to. More working class people dine out, eat takeaways and visit leisure parks, shopping centres and sports arenas, involving similar consumption patterns to the middle class. Foreign travel and holidays have become more available to all where in the 1950s this would be seen as exotic or unusual.

As previous chapters have acknowledged, it can be pointed out as an aspect of this debate that there have been fairly dramatic changes in the class structure, such that there are proportionately fewer members of the traditional working class. Chapters 3 and 5 highlighted the decline in the number of manufacturing factory jobs and the effects of technology on manual occupations. Along with this has been a dramatic expansion in white collar occupations and newer areas of work, which have meant that the old manual/non-manual distinction has become less clear cut. Up to the 1960s sociologists could confidently state that 70 per cent of the population was working class and 30 per cent middle class on a manual/non-manual basis. Now this has become less clear, with some pointing to a much larger proportion of middle class workers, where others suggest that social class alone has become less important than other inequalities such as gender and ethnicity.

Another feature is changes in working patterns and a reduction in hours of work along with the growth of a more shared family life. For example, in the 1940s and 50s most worked on Saturday mornings, so working class men would go to the pub at lunchtime to celebrate the end of the working week and then on to a football match, possibly collecting their son on the way. The 3'o'clock Saturday kick off is a historical reflection of this. Today this is very different with whole families now being encouraged by price reductions to attend.There is now as much fervour from wives and daughters as fathers and sons, with football being described as 'family entertainment'.

Despite such changes it can be still pointed out that class remains as a factor in areas of leisure. At the upper end of the strata, the rich still play and watch polo and horse trials events, and belong to exclusive social and dining clubs. More people of all classes may holiday abroad but there is still a class-based distinction between a holiday in a villa in Tuscany and a fortnight in a hotel in Benidorm. The former holiday includes cultural pursuits such as visiting fortified medieval towns and art galleries, whereas the latter involves the beach and nightclubs. There is a difference in dining out at a pizzeria or a 'Brewer's Fayre' pub and an exclusive restaurant serving French cuisine and expensive wines, which is partly a feature of cost but also one of differing class-based behaviour.

Study point

Investigate among friends and relatives whether their leisure is 'classless' and has no relationship to their occupation.

Activity

Devise a table with Upper, Middle and Working Class and Classless as headings, and list leisure pursuits that are appropriate to each to ascertain whether class is still a factor in leisure opportunities. (This could be developed into a project)

GENDER AND OPPORTUNITIES FOR LEISURE

Leisure is not necessarily an activity, doing nothing, 'staring out of the window' or just sitting down, can all be construed as leisure, especially for houseworkers.

(Rosemary Deem, 'The Politics of Women's Leisure' 1984) Leisure Studies, 1 (1)

The growth in numbers of women in the working population since the mid-twentieth century has been referred to. With reference to leisure opportunities this has meant that increased numbers have earning power which finances a wide range of activities. Along with this has been the extension to the late 20s and 30s of singledom, associated with changed attitudes to marriage and childrearing, meaning that in the younger age range opportunities for leisure for women as well as men have increased.Some may see examples of this in the 1990s emphasis on 'girl power', and 'ladettes' in their late 20s drinking pints of lager in pubs and clubs with their mates. In football, playing and spectatorship has risen dramatically among the female population and this also applies to many other previously 'male only' activities.

Despite such trends it is questionable whether even young women and men are fully equal; parents place more restrictions on their daughters than sons because of fears about safety; young women cannot just go for a walk on their own in a park or the countryside; women runners and cyclists can be subject to sexist verbal harassment from male road users; in formerly male competitive team games women can be subjected to ridicule by male spectators; all these are aspects of a patriarchal society.

Rosemary Deem (1990) stresses the importance of employment in providing money, status and self-confidence for increased numbers of women. Financial independence affects their relationships in that they participate and contribute equally, expecting a say in expenditure. But the idea of equality of opportunity is further brought into question as the majority of women will eventually form relationships and raise children. This severely curtails their opportunity for independent leisure. Modern fathers can also be affected, but in the majority of cases, the woman's career is sacrificed to either full-time childcare until nursery or school age, or part-time employment in the evenings or at weekends. The stereotypical male role of breadwinner returns and the 'working' male sees 'his' leisure as necessary. The loss of a full-time salary and the expense of children can mean less to spend on leisure pursuits. Also for men, opportunities for extra working hours may be taken up, meaning less time for home and family accompanied by tiredness. The 1980s 'New Man', who shared equally in time spent on childcare and household responsibilities, turned out to be a media myth. It is probably true that modern fathers are more involved with their children but this is more likely to be as 'playmates' and entertainment figures to play games with and go out to sports events and cinemas to 'give mum a break'. The everyday care of young children is physically demanding so mothers are likely to use their limited 'free time' to rest with a book or watch television, with perhaps the most active pursuit being shopping. The opportunity for the independent participatory leisure of their youth has disappeared. Deem found that women in her study were acting as chauffeurs, ferrying their children to events and extra-mural classes in music, dancing and sports.

When children grow up and leave home, women are freer to take up leisure pursuits but there are still everyday household tasks to be done after work, with a minority of men contributing equally. Leisure pursuits associated with healthcare and body image such as keep fit and yoga become popular, perhaps reflecting social pressures on women to conform to idealised images.

In the following quote **Eileen Green** et al (1990) point to the male controls, ranging from direct approval or milder sanctioning which steered women into particular 'female' pursuits:

many groups of women are expected to choose their leisure time activities mainly from within the limited range of home and family-oriented activities which are socially defined as acceptable, womanly pursuits.

E. Green, S. Hebron and D. Woodward 'Woman's Leisure, What Leisure?', Macmillan, London 1990

Leisure and the postmodern city

Sheila Scraton and **Peter Bramham** (1999) build on earlier views from feminists such as Deem (1986) that leisure and tourism are male-oriented. They examine differences in male and female leisure 'spaces' by focusing on Leeds in Yorkshire. They were interested in Leeds because, along with a number of other British towns and cities, it has been presented as a '24-hour City' where time boundaries around work, rest and play have been eroded. Note the postmodern features of this perspective: shops and leisure activities open round the clock, supposedly providing a democratic facility for all citizens to participate in a continental-style 'cafe culture' at any time of the day or night. Scraton and Bramham found the reality to be very different. At night Leeds becomes a more frightening and violent place with centre pubs and clubs dominated by heavy drinking and drug-taking young males. They point out that for young working class males much of the formerly factory shopfloor behaviour associated with masculinity and solidarity had shifted to the bars and clubs. There were a number of young females also engaged in similar 'clubbing' activities, but still in a minority. They carried out qualitative interviews with a number of women and found that many, such as the older age group, single parents, black and South Asian working class females did not have access to the pleasures of the '24-hour City'. They found that certain traditional images and roles such as motherhood were still important and leisure activities were associated with this as well as work, such as going out for a drink on payday.

Scraton and Bramham sum up by pointing out:

> *Far from new, 'postmodern' cities providing a democratised leisure setting for the consumption of culture, it remains for many women a gendered and racialised space that offers them few opportunities. These women, in many ways, continue to be marginalised from public 24-hour city leisure and continue to create their own leisure much as many women have always done in local communities and in private spaces.*

S. Scraton, P. Bramham 'Developments in Sociology' (vol 14) Causeway Press (Ormskirk) 1999

ETHNICITY AND LEISURE

Discrimination and prejudice against ethnic minorities is pervasive in all areas of society. The issue of discrimination at work has been examined (Chapter 6). As with class and gender, there can be separateness in leisure pursuits. This can sometimes be identified in terms of cultural differences between white and non-white groups. For example, the majority of Muslims do not drink alcohol on religious grounds so they do not go to pubs. Musical and dance interests can reflect such cultural differences leading to separate leisure for some ethnic groups. However, in many areas of leisure of interest to a wide spectrum there is evidence of discrimination. Young blacks and Asians socialising in the inner city shopping and leisure areas are subject to close surveillance by police and security officials on grounds of their potential for troublemaking and criminality. Older people and their families can be subject to hostile stares in restaurants, sports grounds and the theatre.

In the late 1980s **Scott Fleming** (1993) conducted an ethnographic study in a multi-ethnic school in London to investigate the sports activities of South Asian schoolchildren. At that time the usually white members of sports staff tended to hold negative images of the pupils, seeing them as frail and lacking stamina. In contact sports they could be subject to racist verbal abuse from other pupils. There were fears about safety, particularly in activities outside school hours. Sports dress requirements could sometimes transgress cultural sensitivities regarding modesty in appearance. Parents' disapproval of sports could mean less involvement.

Ellis Cashmore (1982) provides examples of racism in sport that permeates all levels from spectators to players and administrators. There are many role models of black and Asian stars, but they have often achieved their success under severe pressures. They have had to cope with so-called humorous 'banter' and racist name-calling from colleagues. If formal complaints are made, they are accused of over-sensitivity and a lack of 'humour', common cover up strategies for racism experienced in a variety of workplaces. Black footballers are still subjected to racist chants and abuse despite campaigns such as 'Kick Racism Out of Football'. At the school and local level, football is very popular among young Asians. In 1999, media attention focused on Bury, a Second Division club, as they were the first to sign an Asian, an Indian international player. Their Chairman said that he recognised the popularity of football in the Asian community and the potential for added support if they had such a role model.

Despite such possible breakthroughs, in areas with Asian populations there are separate cricket and football leagues and teams. Some professional clubs in such areas are trying to tap into this at the community level as they want to develop stronger links and involve the whole of the population.

In terms of identity for the young and as a reaction to experiences of discrimination and prejudice **Paul Gilroy** (1987) suggests popular culture, music and entertainment become important. Rock music originated from black gospel and blues music. One of the earliest white rock stars, Elvis Presley, was lauded by an impresario as a young white guy who could 'sound like a black rhythm and blues singer'. In his childhood the Presley family lived in a deprived mixed community and the young Elvis sang in the gospel choir in the church his family attended.

Dick Hebdige (1990) has shown how once 'exotic' and ethnically specific forms of music such as reggae become absorbed into mainstream youth culture. In later work, Gilroy (1993) extends this to our pesent day mix of global cultural styles, language, music and dress. From a postmodern perspective such 'crossover' and mix of cultural style may indicate a more optimistic future where ethnicity and difference become unimportant in a generalised search for consumer and leisure-based identity among all young people.

AGE AND LEISURE

Older people tend to have different leisure pursuits to the young as interests change through the life cycle. One obvious factor is that older people have less physical strength to participate in strenuous sports and outdoor pursuits. Young people can sometimes display a form of 'ageism' as they ridicule older age pursuits such as bowling and ballroom dancing. Similarly older people might complain about the leisure pastimes of the young such as loud music and boisterous games and socialising in the street.

Rock music, once exclusively a genre for the young, is now played and listened to by older groups, such that the 'ageing' of rock is being compared to jazz with ever-ageing stars still playing the hits of their youth.

Holidays can be age-segregated and aimed at different groups, such as Club 18–30 for that age group, and Saga holidays for the over 50s.

DISABILITY AND LEISURE

Clearly some disabled persons have physical limitations on their leisure, but in the past disability was a form of social inequality involving assumptions about incapability, stereotyping and labelling in terms of inadequacy. Many sports and leisure centres did not cater for disabled access so, like other discriminated against groups, they were isolated from the leisure pursuits open to others. Shakespeare's (1994) views on the way people have stigmatised the disabled have been examined in an earlier section (see p 86). This can be seen in terms of a 'threat' to 'normal' able-bodied identity.

More recently, many such assumptions have been exposed as incorrect. Disabled people have participated in a wide variety of sports and leisure activities. There is lessening segregation as exemplified by people in wheelchairs competing in marathons along with able-bodied runners. The four-yearly Paralympics occurs after the Olympic Games and now attracts significant media coverage indicating increased levels of acceptance. In 1999 equal opportunities legislation on disability was enacted, accompanied by an advertising campaign pointing out that the disabled were no longer to be kept apart or denied access to work opportunities, leisure and social activities.

SEXUALITY AND LEISURE

Traditionally sexuality and leisure has not been a prominent subject for sociological study but recently this topic has featured consistently in the mass media. As pointed out by Scraton (1992) and **Arthur Brittan** (1989) high speed, strenuous physical contact sports such as boxing, rugby and football have been associated with particular images of aggressive masculine identity. Behavioural expectations include sexism accompanied by virulent anti-gay or homophobic attitudes. Clearly with such activities, being homosexual causes difficulties. Until recently players of such sports had to keep homosexual identity secret for fear of ridicule and violence. Justin Fashanu, a football star of the early 1990s, eventually committed suicide after an unhappy life of depression and drug-taking. Some see change in the situation of gay people in sport. In tennis female stars such as Martina Navratilova were open about being gay. Similar outings have occurred in a wide range of sports. However the situation of wealthy professional stars may be exceptional compared with a young man or woman involved in local amateur sport where the old prejudices prevail, leading to fear and secretiveness.

Another dimension is that of gender expectations where women playing 'men's' sports are labelled as 'butch' or 'unfeminine', and men involved in 'feminine' activities such as dancing are ridiculed in terms of their sexuality.

In professional entertainment, until recently, gay male stars kept their sexual identity secret, particularly if their career was based on their attractiveness to the opposite sex. Some had 'fake' marriages and girlfriends. The 1950s heart-throb, Rock Hudson, was an attractive looking man, whose death from AIDS in the early 1990s caused consternation. Even outrageously 'camp' entertainers, such as the cross-dressing Danny La Rue, presented a heterosexual facade in his life outside showbusiness. Another more recent strategy, used by Boy George early in his career, was to emphasise asexual and celibate private lives when the truth was very different.

Now stars such as Elton John and George Michael can be open about their sexual proclivities without affecting their record sales. Eddie Izzard is openly transvestite, and Julian Clary has an act centred around his homosexuality. Soap operas have featured lesbian love scenes, all perhaps indicating a changed climate regarding the portrayal of sexuality.

However, the rich and famous may be able to be more open and less fearful (although Eddie Izzard was attacked in the street a few years ago), but in everyday leisure and sport there are probably many who are fearful of openness because of similar prejudices and discrimation to those faced by other oppressed groups.

THE LEISURE INDUSTRY

From the 1960s, the move toward increased opportunities for leisure led to the development of increasingly large entertainment, sports and leisure corporations run by high profile figures such as Rupert Murdoch and Richard Branson who became seen as the new generation of capitalists, making fortunes in similar ways to the major manufacturers and industrialists of previous times. From a neo-Marxist perspective Clarke and Critcher (1985) see such developments as part of the capitalist process which is constantly seeking new ways to make profits at the expense of the working class. Such neo-capitalists as Murdoch and Branson now run vast global empires, taking over every aspect of the entertainment and sports industries. After originally establishing himself with Virgin Records, founded on the success of Mike Oldfield's phenomenally successful 1970s album 'Tubular Bells', Richard Branson is now so successful that he has diversified into air and rail travel, banking and insurance. His more recent ventures include 'cola' drinks and clothing.

The football club Manchester United have become a global corporation which is now moving into the lucrative 'pay per view' digital TV market. Fortunes have been made from merchandising of branded clothing and sportswear. Recently a director sold a proportion of his shares for over £40 million. There have been protests at the expense of constantly changing football strips. Some London clubs now charge over £30 to spectators which could mean a bill of up to £100 for a family, a large outlay compared with other forms of entertainment. Some predict that some of this over-zealous profiteering is beginning to backfire as attendances at Premier League matches started to fall in the 1999–2000 season. Critics of so-called class domination theory such as Roberts (1984) advocate a pluralist view, pointing to the enormous diversity of leisure and sports options, some of them expensive and perhaps exploitative of the working class, but many others cheap or free such as walking in the countryside or a local park. Cheaper leisure activities in recreational parks and sports grounds are funded by the state and benefit a wide range of social classes, women, ethnic minorities and the disabled, counteracting neo-Marxist views of unbridled capitalist profiteering.

POSTMODERN EXPLANATIONS OF LEISURE

Postmodernists emphasise the fragmentary and less predictable nature of our social lives in modern times. They see old forms of social identity and inequality such as class, gender and ethnicity as increasingly less important in a fluid, rapidly changing society. They point to consumption as a key to explaining new forms of identity which transcend others. For example, age stratification was once seen in terms of separateness between the young, the middle-aged and the old in terms of interests, appearance and dress. Now these differences have become blurred with the middle-aged and elderly wearing T-shirts and jeans and listening to rock music.

Consumption and brand names have become an aspect of identity as we spend our leisure time in vast shopping complexes, the modern 'cathedrals of consumption'. From the outside the Trafford Centre, Manchester, resembles a gothic cathedral combined with a renaissance palace. Inside, as well as the shops and stores, there are multiplex cinemas, restaurants and bars, replicas of ocean-going liners, Egyptian pyramids and classical sculptures. There are high-tech fun and adventure activities for children, the aim being to provide for 'all the family'. The Trafford Centre is a clear example of what **Jean-Paul Baudrillard** (1988) described as 'hyper-reality'. Someone from another culture or society would probably be perplexed in terms of how to categorise such a centre offering play and entertainment, eating and drinking, as well as shopping for brand-name goods. The leisure group 'Centreparcs' have provided another example of 'hyper-reality' with their covered enclosed holiday centres where even the vagaries of the British climate can be overcome as we sit by a tropical pool sipping an ice cold drink under a live palm tree.

In popular music since the 1980s there has been increased recycling of previous fashions and styles from the 1960s and 70s. Ageing stars such as Tom Jones and Tony Bennett suddenly become fashionable and trendy and record with younger bands. There have been debates about whether such ageing sex symbols are embarrassing parodies of their younger selves. Some accounts suggest postmodern themes of irony and pastiche where the stars take a 'tongue in cheek' attitude to their renewed fame. Tom Jones has said that the women's knickers that get thrown at him have become larger as his audience has aged!

Another recent phenomenon is the growth of tribute bands such as the 'Rolling Clones' and the 'Bootleg Beatles'. Some of these are judged to be better than the originals. The Australian Abba tribute band 'Bjorn Again' do year-round sell-out tours and have recently celebrated their tenth anniversary without selling a single record. The Oasis tribute band 'No Way Sis' were playing live versions of a new CD track before the real band had had a chance to perform it. Such a confusing, chaotic world provides an image which illustrates postmodern themes of change and the future.

Postmodern studies of leisure have highlighted the changing leisure patterns and identified issues around consumption, images and lifestyle. Veal (1993) sees postmodern themes in research which investigates the ways individuals and social groups construct life style and express leisure tastes. Postmodern consumers are spoilt for choice and construct identities around consumption patterns. We no longer shop for necessities alone but construct global identities from the supermarket shelves where curries and Italian pasta can be accompanied by authentic fruit and vegetables from the countries of origin. Pizzerias advertising 'Halal Pizzas' in their window reflect postmodern themes of blurred cross-cultural boundaries. Computer technology means you can have limitless experiences without leaving your armchair. Virtual reality machines can simulate travel and participation in sports. You can become a champion Grand Prix driver on a machine in your local pub. With a CD-ROM you can visit major art galleries such a the Louvre without travelling to Paris. **John Urry** (1990) shows how tourism has developed in an increasingly polarised and divided society. For a privileged few, there is a quest for the increasingly exotic and unusual. We seek ever new experiences and can relive history through 'living museums', 'authentic' settings of Victorian schoolrooms, mines and Viking settlements, peopled by actors in appropriate costumes who interact with us to convey the 'real' experience.

SUMMARY

This chapter has examined an increasingly important aspect of our lives in modern societies. Sociologists from the 1970s on have studied the role of leisure in society. Early approaches showed how attitudes to work affected leisure. Links were made between stages of the family life cycle and leisure patterns. Others pointed to the massive expansion of opportunities possibly resulting in a 'democracy of leisure' compensating for unfulfilling work for many. Conflict sociologists have taken issue with ideas of democratic or equal opportunities for leisure. They point to inequalities along familiar lines of social class, ethnicity and gender. More recently issues of age, disability and sexuality have been examined in relation to leisure. The development of a highly commercialised 'leisure industry' making vast profits for a 'new capitalist' class, as has happened with football, has been highlighted. More recent postmodern ideas of leisure combining with culture and identity in the products we consume have shed light on social changes in such a significant area of our lives.

STUDY GUIDE

Group work

1 Class to divide into females and males. List the variety of leisure activities engaged in to see if leisure is different along gender lines. Are males freer than females? What about available leisure time? Parental controls? Safety and security?
2 Discuss the view that leisure is freer for men than women.

Practice questions

1 Evaluate the view that work affects leisure patterns.
2 'Ethnic minorities face discrimination in their leisure'. Discuss.
3 Examine sociological explanations of women's leisure.
4 Assess the view that leisure has become more democratic.
5 'Leisure is now a vast capitalist industry.' Discuss.

Coursework

Clearly leisure provides much opportunity for coursework. Be careful of trivialised or unsociological descriptive study such as pop music or unethical areas such as drinking or illegal drug-taking among the young as a leisure pursuit. Be aware that football is a very popular topic so choose a more unusual angle. 'Clubbing' as a topic is best avoided.

1 Conduct an investigation using a survey of young people and their leisure. Identify possible class, gender and ethnic differences.
2 Conduct an oral history project with old people to investigate their leisure when they were your age.
3 If you are a member of a sports or social club you could investigate other members to find out the reasons for their choice and interests.
4 What examples are there in your area of a leisure industry? Investigate how important this is to the community.
5 Examine similar versions of 'hyper-reality' to the examples on p 00 to investigate postmodern themes and approaches to leisure.

10

THE FUTURE OF WORK, LEISURE AND UNEMPLOYMENT

Introduction

As we start the third millennium it is clear we are entering a phase of dramatic change in the way we live our lives. Work, leisure and economic life will alter dramatically and everyone will be affected. The most significant change is already occurring as a shift away from the permanence of full-time work and a career for life becomes the norm for the majority of the population. Permanent and stable life course careers have declined for increased numbers as technology and the information revolution increasingly impinge on all aspects of our lives in ways unimagined by previous generations.

The close of the twentieth century might be seen as the end of work as we have known it from the early onset of industrialisation. Some see the emergence of a 'post-industrial' society where computers and the realm of information technology have blown apart our previously stable working lives. 'What do you do?' as a question about identity associated with work becomes increasingly irrelevant. This raises issues of culture and identity – another aspect of newer developments in the sociological syllabus.

This final chapter raises a number of possibly speculative points about the future of work, leisure and unemployment based on economic and social trends examined throughout this book. There is no doubt that we are living through 'revolutionary' times every bit as eventful as previous agricultural and industrial revolutions which so dramatically affected the lives of our distant ancestors.

EDUCATIONAL AND TRAINING CHANGES

The tiny proportion of school leavers entering permanent full-time work is evidence of such changes. Correspondingly, the numbers continuing education and training to well beyond the school leaving age, many to degree and higher educational levels, means that the age of first entering employment is rising. Currently, universities are focusing on a policy of flexible degrees where students can enter and leave, building a portfolio of qualifications over a number of years. This would end the full-time three-year degree for all but a minority. Reasons for such a policy can be seen in the implementation of student tuition fees and the decline of the grant for full-time study. Increased numbers of young people could be in their late 20s and early 30s before entering the full-time labour market having previously interspersed periods of full- or part-time temporary employment (shopwork, fast food, catering, hotel and tourism) with periods of full- or part-time 'flexible' study to build up a qualifications and training portfolio.

THE CHANGING CONTEXT OF WORK

Chapter 5 highlighted several aspects of this. One current debate focuses on the spread of home computing and telecommunications. Some envisage that this will rapidly increase, making it possible for large numbers to work from home. This pattern is already emerging with many staying at home for much of the week, attending their office on one or two days. The mobile phone and laptop computer have meant that work is not bound to a particular place. Internet conferencing will reduce the need for travel.

The growth of homeworking is seen as a potentially liberating force for many who in the past were denied opportunities to go out to work. Women with young children and the disabled are examples here. Critics point to the possibility of low-paid exploitation which has been a long term feature of homeworking. There are also issues of loneliness and isolation which can affect homeworkers. Going out to work can provide indirect social benefits such as relationships within teams or groups of workers in offices, factories and shops. There is also a sense of time and structure in the 9–5 working week.

However, some also see benefits from the opportunity to work at home coming from reductions in commuter travel. We are all familiar with the destructive effects of rush hour travel, and there are worrying projections for ever-increasing traffic volumes. The expansion of homeworking will possibly ameliorate this.

Despite such projections it needs to be pointed out that the majority will continue to go out to work for some time. Technological innovations may benefit particular groups of more middle class workers such as managers and professionals, but goods still have to be made in factories which may become more automated but still require human input. Home shopping on the Internet is now available but there are still many expanding shopping and consumer complexes needing armies of workers. We can now have home cinema entertainment centres with surround sound but more are going out to see films in multiplex cinemas and having meals in associated restaurants afterwards.

The effect of current work trends on character, commitment and personal lives

Richard Sennett (1998) an American sociologist has studied changing trends through the generations. He argues that despite so-called 'improvements' in pay, working conditions, opportunities and associated standards of living there are a number of negative factors brought about by flexibility, innovation and risk. One key feature of his work is that there has been a decline in commitment and loyalty to companies, perhaps unsurprising in times of insecure and shifting patterns of employment. Sennett sees a development from this in terms of the 'corrosion of character' which affects personal relationships outside work. Evidence is seen in rocketing divorce rates and relationship breakdown. There is frequent publicity about male lack of commitment to permanent relationships which he links to the changed work situation where impermanency and insecurity abound. In the past rigid, heirarchical organisations could be oppressive and exploitative in familiar ways, but a sense of personal character and commitment was developed in such contexts. He sees current dynamic, flexible and rapidly changing trends as destructive of aspects of character in terms of sustained purpose, integrity of self, and trust in others, all detrimental to our personal lives.

Modern management culture and technology

Richard Scase (1998) has doubts whether technological developments will result in a massive shift to homeworking. He points out that modern management culture insists that employees come to work on a regular basis. This ensures face-to-face supervision to ensure compliance in carrying out tasks and duties. Sociologists point out that societies are made up of social structures consisting of traditions, cultures and power relationships. Factors such as these shape the take-up of developments in information technology and, hence, the future of work. He concludes that it is unlikely that there will be a revolution in work practices on the scale predicted by many contemporary technology gurus.

Study point

What do you think your future work context will be? Would you prefer to work from home? Compare the advantages and disadvantages of homeworking with going out to work.

CURRENT TRENDS IN WORK AND LEISURE

There are a number of terms that have been increasingly used to illustrate changing patterns in our working and leisure lives:

- **Downsizing/rightsizing**

  An example of this is where Japanese-style methods have been applied to create teams of workers who make decisions about how they work. This has lessened the need for external supervision by chargehands and managers. Such lower and middle management has been shed making 'leaner, fitter' companies which are able to adapt and change quickly to new market situations. Such trends aim to create efficiency by more effective and democratic communication, lessening the need for labour-intensive bureaucracy.

- **Outsourcing**

  This is where previously large companies scale down their operations by using networks of smaller companies to make components which might need to be changed quickly. In the car industry, parts such as lights may be outsourced to a smaller manufacturer. An advantage is that globalised networks mean that cheaper components can be sought in low wage economies.

- **'New Age' Management Culture**

  British companies through the 1990s increasingly adopted aspects of American managerial practices, McDonalds being one example. Another is Total Quality Management (TQM) where the whole organisation becomes involved in improving quality, worker empowerment and client/customer focus. This ethos is visible in a wide range of workplaces serving the public with proudly displayed customer charters, mission statements and quality kitemarks in hospital and doctor's waiting rooms, garages, travel agencies, and schools, colleges and universities. It is stressed that the most important person in the organisation is the one who first meets the customer so porters, cleaners and receptionists are drawn in and sent on TQM courses.

Those who have taken up such themes for their for their organisations encourage attendance on courses provided by American TQM companies where an atmosphere of evangelical zeal is fostered getting across quasi-religious messages to 'improve Quality' and 'empower your workforce' which are displayed as icon-like slogans.

- **Downshifting**

  Some, usually middle class professionals, have reacted to increased pressures and stresses in work by opting out and seeking less pressurised lives. There has been media publicity about some 'high-fliers' who have taken this course which might be the equivalent of earlier notions of 'dropping out'. Along with changing to less stressful, possibly home-based work there has been a reaction to extravagant consumption and ecological concerns. The phrase 'downshifting into voluntary simplicity' was taken up enthusiastically by such groups in America as middle-class professionals (see Work-Rich/Time Poor below)

Activity
Find out where your school or college charters and mission statements are displayed. What do they mean? Discuss with a manager such as a year head.

- **Workaholism**
  This connects with 'Downshifting' and 'Work-Rich/Time-Poor' where increased numbers particularly in management and professional occupations, not only have external pressures to work longer hours from employers,but also develop internal personality characteristics that drive them to continue working at all hours of the day or night.Clearly computer technology has added to this where work can be taken home outside office hours. (Although there was recent publicity about an American company which now opens until late evenings and has provided a rest/sleep room where employees can 'recharge their batteries'.) The growth of work stress-related illnesses is perhaps evidence of the 'workaholic' culture among certain groups. **Juliet Schor** (1991) has provided an economic background to this by showing that if we had the same standard of living as in 1948, current productivity levels would mean an average 4 hour day.

- **Work-Rich/Time-Poor**
  Increased numbers of highly paid professional couples are working longer hours for huge salaries and joint household income. This is used to buy snatched non-work and leisure time and employ groups of domestic and childcare workers. Some are beginning to question such lifestyles and may see 'downshifting' as an option. Critics point to the polarisation between these workers and the large numbers trapped in low wage, insecure and unfulfilling work, who have the opposite problem,Work-Poor/Time-Rich.

- **Polarisation**
  It has been argued that the future will see a widening gap between the working 'haves' and the non-working 'have nots'. The former will be working longer hours. Handy (1994) demonstrates that 100,000 hours of the traditional 45-year working life is now being squeezed into 30 years, a period in which there is precious little time for anything else but work. Far from the predicted 30-hour week for everyone, by the start of the twenty-first century it is more likely that half the workforce will be putting in 60 hours and a great many of

the rest will have no work at all. Such trends, if fully materialised, will be detrimental for women who need work hours to be spread over a longer career lifetime.

EVALUATION

Advocates of some of the trends identified above see an exciting, more democratic future in work organisations where work for all becomes more productive, involving and fulfilling. Nobody would disagree with the idea that customer service should be improved. However, there are issues raised by critics. One concerns defining 'quality', which can be an amorphous concept which becomes meaningless. Another is that improvements based on 'evangelical zeal' are often short term, with exponents recognising that there is a constant need to reinvigorate with fresh issues to be addressed on a regular basis.

Conflict sociologists point out that such approaches reflect an increasingly competitive market and business environment where supposed 'empowerment' involves increased commitment and productivity. Workers are encouraged to wear uniforms and develop a Japanese-style 'corporate identity', another aspect of their increased commitment. They see such developments as being to do with masking inequalities and business problems in a rapidly changing globalised economic climate. Many workers are under the threat of redundancy and required to work harder for the same or less pay. The new situation is that this is affecting all types of occupation. Now the manager, teacher, social worker and university lecturer face the same insecurities of employment as factory workers have previously done.

FUTURE TRENDS

Sociologists range from those who see cause for optimism in the future to those who see a more bleak, darker picture.

Probably the most optimistic portrait is the functionalist one. There are a number of features of this approach:

- developments in technology will lead to more automated production which will replace the more monotonous, low-skilled work;
- workers now have increased opportunities to retrain and update educational qualifications. This enhances their job opportunities and leads to the possibility of more fulfilling work;
- work will become less central to people's lives and fulfilment will come from other things, such as a contented family life and leisure, sport and travel;
- there will be more flexibility and choice in working lives such as jobshare schemes and flexitime arrangements where people can construct their own

working timetables which gives more power and control. Handy (1984) sees these as desirable options for a more democratic working life where work hours can be tailored to suit home and family commitments;

- following from postmodern ideas, boundaries between work and leisure and other aspects of our lives will become increasingly blurred as more work from home using computers and telecommunications. Using a computer can involve dimensions of communication such as E-Mail where fun messages to friends and relatives can be interspersed with work-related activity. The Internet can be a useful tool for work information as well as having a 'play' dimension, perhaps summed up in the phrase 'surfing the net'.

More pessimistic views of the future come from a conflict perspective which doubts some of the more optimistic projections above:

- technology may eradicate some monotonous work but will lead to unemployment or unfulfilling jobs in the low-skilled service industries such as shopwork and catering. For example, a redundant factory worker replaced by robot technology may end up stacking shelves in a supermarket or working as a security guard for minimum wage rates;
- the need for skills updating and retraining will mean longer periods in education, resulting in financial hardship as grants become reduced and fees charged. Students are already taking out loans and running into debts which take a long time to pay off;
- the so-called empowerment and choice in work is illusory. For many there are increased requirements from working at home which can mean you are never switched off from work, there is always 'something to do'. The European minimum working time directive which advocates a 48-hour maximum working week has aroused controversy as it has excluded certain occupations in administration, management and the professions.It was felt that a 48-hour maximum was too restrictive for such workers who need to be flexible in their working hours. It was pointed out that many such occupations involve working at home where hours worked are difficult to monitor;
- leisure, family life and personal relationships may become more important than work,but work provides a vital source of income which if low leads to exclusion from access to the more pleasurable leisure and family-related activities. Many would still see satisfying well-paid work as an essential feature of a full life which can qualitatively affect our personal and private lives;
- Marxists see economic and technological developments as maintaining capitalist interests.

As has been previously discussed, the leisure 'industry' makes huge profits for the 'new capitalists' and relies on an often low-skilled, low paid workforce. The 'deskilling debate' highlighted the way technology can replace and disempower workers who are either left to unemployment as part of the 'reserve army of labour' or working in the insecure low wage economy.

Postmodern predictions of future trends

These are rooted in the present and see the current fragmentation of work and the blurring of work and non-work boundaries as continuing. Whether such trends will lead to a better future is open to doubt. Some will benefit from a high tech future, developing their creative skills in a context of high financial rewards and flexibility, with choice and power over their work-related activities. However, there will be increased polarisation as there will be a large group of excluded workers who either become long-term unemployed or forced into the low wage, insecure service economy. The old joke about what you say to a university graduate, 'A Big Mac and French Fries please', although exaggerated, may well be the future for some. Certain groups may benefit. There is evidence that women are increasingly becoming the key and most desirable workers as they cope with the demands of flexible, more fluid working arrangements better than men who are entrenched in 'old' expectations of a career and 'job for life'. Women are now proportionately half the workforce and this is expected to rise so that women will become a majority. There are now more young female solicitors than male, and more than half of current medical students are female.

Other groups, such as the disabled, will have greater opportunities from technological advances giving access to workplaces or the chance to work from home using computers and modern telecommunications.

In the area of leisure and consumption the spending power of gay people has become recognised as the 'pink pound' has led to the development of gay 'villages' in many towns and cities with bars, clubs, shops and restaurants catering for this previously hidden, ghettoised group.There are now holiday resorts catering for a gay clientele.

A GLOBALIZED DIVISION OF LABOUR?

Another dimension of the postmodern approach is the debate concerning globalisation. Here the boundaries between countries and nation states are seen as having less importance. Huge transnational or international corporations have extended their influence throughout the world. Many were originally American-owned and based such as Ford, IBM, Coca-Cola and McDonalds.

F. Froebel (1980) points to the enormous influence such corporations have had on international labour patterns. The old division of labour, where colonies in Africa and Asia provided raw materials which were transported to the manufacturing industries in the colonial industrial countries in the West, has changed. Many previously-described Third World countries are now independent and have established their own manufacturing base. This has become attractive to transnational corporations because in labour-intensive production, wage costs are much cheaper in countries with a low standard of living. Added benefits are that worker representation via trade unions is usually less established or, in some dictatorships, banned. This avoids a so-called 'troublesome' workforce pressurising for higher pay and better conditions. The result has been an expansion of manufacturing jobs in such countries and a resultant dramatic decline in manufacturing jobs in countries such as Britain.

Current trends in globalisation

From the 1960s Japan dominated Asia to become one of the world's leading industrial nations.From the 1980s the fastest growing economies have been the 'Tiger' or 'Pacific Rim' economies to be found in countries and regions such as Taiwan, Malaysia, South Korea, Hong Kong and Singapore. In East Asia economic growth averaged 7.5 per cent between 1974 and 1993. In the developed world the equivalent figure was 2.9 per cent. The World Bank forecasts that the developing world will provide 60 per cent of output by 2020 compared with 35 per cent from the developed world, almost reversing the situation prevailing in the mid-twentieth century.

Some countries have had phenomenal spurts in their productive capacity where output has doubled within a decade. The next development is expected to be from China whose manufacturing output has risen dramatically during the 1990s. With such a large population providing a cheap labour force and a gigantic home market for consumer goods, the predictions are that China will become the world's major economic power within a few years of the twenty-first century.

Paul Kennedy (1996) points to the detrimental effects of a globalised labour market on low-paid workers in the European Union and the USA whose jobs are increasingly threatened by manufactured goods produced elsewhere. In manufacturing, consumer goods trends in globalisation have meant that it is increasingly difficult to identify a product with a particular country. In car production, a 'British' or 'Japanese' car could be made of components from a range of countries; Japanese companies setting up in Britain as car 'manufacturers' in fact are using British labour as assemblers of components manufactured elsewhere; a Ford or Volvo car can often be a globally produced product. So identity of origin for a product is becoming less associated with a country or nation.

Grint (1999) examines the impact of globalization on work and identifies a number of features and trends. He identifies some elements of convergence in the globalised trading and working structures. For example, Japanese working practices have been adopted but moulded to the American and European cultural context. American-influenced managerial practices such as Total Quality Management (TQM see p 57) have been taken up with a change in organisations to a 'customer' focus, with an emphasis on quality and flexibility in approach. Rather than one managerial style, he sees a range from the 'hard' as with Mcdonalds, to the 'soft' where flexibility, decision-making and the use of skills are developed in a 'flatter' organisational structure.

In a section on globalisation and novelty, Grint points out that a number of features are not new. There has been a form of 'globalised' interaction for centuries with trade, military and religious expansion. The British East India Company which transported goods to and from the Asian sub-continent was established by Elizabeth I in 1600.

However, there are some qualitative differences between the past and present. Knowledge has become more significant than things or concrete manufactured products. As Giddens (1990) has pointed out, information technology has resulted in 'time-space distantiation' where global communications in areas such as financial markets have become 24-hour. There are now 'virtual companies' on the Internet with no national boundaries.

Nation states have been predicted as becoming less influential but without some form of effective world monitoring and governance are still important in areas of economic, business and financial activity and decisions. Multinational Corporations (MNCs) do not have unbridled power; they often have to accommodate and adapt to local issues.

Grint examines the effect of globalisation on job security. In 1996 the *Observer* noted that 40 per cent of the working population feared for their jobs with a further 60 per cent feeling rising insecurity. Staff are now less committed to their organisations, but the proportion with tenure (long-term contracts) has not altered dramatically. Now 28 per cent are in part-time jobs compared with 5 per cent in the 1950s. In 1996 57 per cent of the British workforce were in full-time jobs. In banking, the 444,800 workforce in 1990 were reduced to 363,000 in 1995, working in half the number of branches. Pessimists such as Rifkin (1995) see the end of work such that as the industrialisation of agriculture saw the end of the horse: the computerisation of work will see the end of the human. Grint develops Marx's view that capitalism produces its own gravedigger in the proletariat by adding that the proletariat digs its own grave and jumps in to be covered by a robot! However, he concludes that we are 'a long way from assuming that globalisation has finally begun the end of work; there is simply too much to do.'

1   Investigate the effects of globalisation by examining a range of products such as clothing, electronic goods and cars. Where were they manufactured? What are the wages and standards of living there? Are any products identifiably British? What are they? Explain in the context of globalisation.

2   'Britain is no longer a manufacturing nation.' Discuss.

SUMMARY

The start of a new century raises thoughts about what may happen in the next 100 years. In this book the topic of work and leisure clearly indicates that change is inevitable. There seem to be a range of indications that postmodern ideas of fragmentation, flexibility and blurring of work and non-work boundaries is already here. Will this leave scope for new forms of non-work identity through leisure and consumption, eroding old divisions of social class which were based on occupation? It is possible that the vision of D.H. Lawrence in the following extract might become the norm:

What is He?

What is he?
– a man, of course
Yes, but what does he do?
– He lives and is a man
Oh, quite! But he must work –
he must have a job of some sort.
– Why?

'What is He?' DH Lawrence, selected poems (ed) Mara Kalnins, Everyman Library, Dent, 1992

Group work

1 A good activity enabling brainstorming and imagination to complete this Work and Leisure module is to prepare a presentation, accompanied by posters and displays, which addresses the future. In small groups select a topic from: the Future of Work; the Future of Leisure; Changes in Management and Organisation of Work; the Effects of Globalisation on Work; Work for Women and Men; Work for Ethnic Minorities; the Disabled and Different Age Groups; Future Patterns of Leisure and Non-Work Activities; the Role of Technology in Our Future Working Lives. Each group to research (you could even use futuristic accounts such as science fiction) and do a class presentation ideally accompanied by flipchart posters which can be used as wall displays.

2 Using the D.H. Lawrence extract above as a starting point, discuss with others and make a list of the qualities that might identify a person other than their occupation.

Practice questions

1 What impact will computer technology have on work in the future?
2 Discuss the view that work will become more fragmented and flexible for future generations.
3 Examine the effects of current trends on unemployment.
4 Assess whether leisure will become increasingly important in the future.
5 What is the impact of globalisation on work?

Coursework suggestions

Use sections of this book as a background for a research project on the future. Design a small social survey and include a range of age, class, gender and ethnic backgrounds to elicit perceptions of work and leisure in the future. It would be good to interview parents of young children to gauge their views on what might be their child's future in terms of work and related themes such as education.

FURTHER READING AND RESOURCES

You may need to carry more detailed reading to complement your study of this book. The following are some suggestions which are probably available from your teacher or the library. There are a number of empirical studies which have been outlined in this book which you may find useful for coursework ideas. Journals such as Sociology Review can be subscribed to you if you want to keep up to date with developments (ask your teacher). Do not be overwhelmed, select what seems interesting and manageable. Even teachers and authors(!) cannot read everything:

BOOKS AND JOURNAL ARTICLES

Beynon, H., Working for Ford (1975, Allen Lane, Harmondsworth)

Blackwell, T. and Seabrook, J., Talking Work: an Oral History (1996, Faber and Faber, London)

Crompton, R., Women and Work in Modern Britain (1997, Oxford University Press, Oxford)

Deem, R., All Work and No Play: the Sociology of Women and Leisure (1986, Open University Press, Milton Keynes)

Duncombe, J. and Marsden, D., Women's 'triple shift' in Sociology Review 4(4) 1995

Elliot, J., 'What do women want? Women, work and the Hakim debate' in Sociology Review 6(4) 1997

Fleming, S., 'Schooling, sport and ethnicity: a case study' in Sociology Review 3(1) 1993

Franks, S., Having none of it: Women, Men and the Future of Work (1999, Granta, London)

Grint, K., The Sociology of Work, an introduction (1991, Polity Press, Cambridge)

Haralambos, M. and Holborn, M., Sociology: Themes and Perspectives 5th edition (2000, Collins Educational, London)

Jorgensen, N., et al., Sociology: an Interactive Approach (1997, Collins Educational, London)

Leonard, P., 'Gender and Organisations' in M. Haralambos (ed) Developments in Sociology vol. 14 (1999, Causeway Press, Ormskirk)

Pollert, A., Girls, Wives, Factory Lives (1981, Macmillan, Basingstoke)

Ritzer, G., The McDonaldization of Society (1993, Pine Forge Press, Thousand Oaks)

Scase, R., 'The Future of Work' in Sociology Review 8(2) 1998

Scraton, S. and Bramham, P., 'Leisure in the Postmodern City' in M. Haralambos (ed)

Developments in Sociology vol. 14 (1999, Causeway Press, Ormskirk)

Shakespeare, T., 'Disabled People: dustbins for disavowal?' in Disability and Society 9(3) 1994

Thompson, P. and McHugh, D., Work Organisations: a Critical Introduction 2nd edition (1995, Macmillan, London)
Webster, F. 'The Information Society?' in Sociology Review 7(2) 1997
Westwood, S., All Day, Every Day: Factory and Family in the Making of Women's Lives (1984, Pluto Press, London)

WEB SITES

Those with access to the Internet and the World Wide Web can access a huge range of information on this rapidly developing resource. To start try:

Electronic Journal of Sociology on http://gpu.srv.ualberta.ca.8010/home1.html
Association for the Teaching of the Social Sciences (ATSS)
<http:/www.le.ac.uk/education/cenres/ATSS/atss.html>
WWW Virtual Library: Sociology http://www.fisk.edu/vl/Sociology/Overview.html
The Socioweb http://www.socioweb.com/-markbl/socioweb/
Sociosite http://www.pscw.uva.nl/sociosite/index.html
Social Science 'Index' on http://www.yahoo.com/

INDEX

Adhocracy 63
Age Hierarchy 85–6, 124
Alienation 18–19, 38, 40, 43–4, 97, 98
Anomie 20, 22
Assembly lines 35, 43–4, 54, 97, 98

Barron and Norris 36–7
Beynon, Huw 43–4
Blauner, Robert 40–41
Braverman, Harry J 44–7
Bureaucracies 25, 37–8, 58–60
Burnham, James 16, 30–31

Capitalism 14–15, 16, 22–4, 29, 44, 53, 58, 62, 68
Clarke and Critcher 19, 126
Class 68–9, 82, 83, 118–19
Class conflict 15, 38, 62, 118–19
Clegg Stuart 63–4
Conditions and Pay 71–2, 78
Conflict theory 17, 18, 31, 38, 135

Davis and Moore 27
Deem, Rosemary 121
Democratisation of Leisure 117
Deskilling 20, 39, 44–7, 56
Division of Labour 20–21, 25
Dual Labour Market 36–7, 74
Durkheim, Emile 20–22

Engels, Friedrich 15, 53
Ethnicity 36, 47, 81–4, 102, 105, 122–4

'Fat Cats' 29–30
Feminism 53, 73–4, 101
Flexible Production 54–5
Ford and Fordism 54
Functionalism 26–7, 28–9, 43, 95, 135–6

Gender Inequality 36, 47, 73–4, 120–22
Globalisation 99, 137–9
Goffman, Erving 61–2
Goldthorpe and Lockwood 41–2
Grint, Keith 41, 139

Hakim, Catherine 75–8

Industrial action 93–8

Job Segregation 74–5

Managerial Revolution 16, 30–31
Manual/Non-Manual Work 68–71
Marx/Marxism 14–20, 25, 26, 38, 58, 62, 68, 73, 99, 101
McDonaldization 56–7
Mead, Margaret 85–6
Meritocracy 28

Neo-Marxism 40, 43, 83, 95, 96, 103, 126
Neo-Weberian Theory 42, 56, 60, 84
Non-Work 115

Organisations Theory 60

Polarisation 47, 134
Post-feminism 75–8
Post-Fordism 54–5
Postmodernism 63–4, 123–4, 126–8, 137

Rationalisation 25
Reserve Army of Labour 19–21, 68, 74, 83

Scraton and Bramham 122
Skills/Reskilling 27, 46, 47, 103, 104
Smith, Adam 20–21
Social Determinism 42
Status 26, 64
Stratification 25–6, 27–8

Taylor and Cohen 97–8
Technological Determinism 40–41, 42–3
Total Institutions 61–2
Trade Unions 98–9

Underclass 109

Weber/Weberian Theory 22–6, 37, 58–60
Women's 'Choices' 75–8

Youth 123–4